W9-AHR-687

Words for the Journey

Letters to Our Teenagers about Life and Faith—REVISED AND UPDATED

MARTIN B. COPENHAVER and ANTHONY B. ROBINSON

Foreword by William H. Willimon

THE PILGRIM PRESS
CLEVELAND

This book is dedicated to our children

ALANNA

JOSEPH

LAURA

NICK

TODD

and to all of our children by baptism.

The Pilgrim Press, 700 Prospect Avenue, Cleveland, Ohio 44115-1100
pilgrimpress.com
© 2003, 2011 by Martin B. Copenhaver and Anthony B. Robinson

Unless otherwise noted, biblical quotations are from the New Revised Standard Version of the Bible, © 1989 by the Division of Christian Education of the National Council of the Churches of Christ in the U.S.A. and are used by permission. Adaptations have been made for inclusivity.

All rights reserved. First edition 2003
Revised and updated edition 2011

Printed in the United States of America on acid-free paper

This book has been reproduced as a digital reprint.

Library of Congress Cataloging-in-Publication Data

Copenhaver, Martin B., 1954–
    Words for the journey : letters to our teenagers about life and death / Martin B. Copenhaver and Anthony B. Robinson ; foreword by William H. Willimon.
      p. cm.
    ISBN 978-0-8298-1888-8 (revised edition)
    ISBN 0-8298-1564-3 (pbk. : alk. paper)
    1. Christian teenagers—Religious life. 2. Christianity—Miscellanea. I. Robinson, Anthony B. II. Title.
BV4531.3.C67 2003
248.8'3—dc21   2003051402

CONTENTS

Foreword

Here is a good book of good advice by two good fathers to (based upon what I've heard from their fathers) two good young people. And what greater need have two aspiring adults than some parental advice? After all, the way to Christian discipleship, the road to life, is not that easy to find on your own. Thus, parental advice.

In principle, I agree with Roy Blount, who says, "My advice to young people is, don't listen to advice. I say this not only because it is something that young people will listen to. I say it also because questionable advice ("Hey, organic chemistry will take care of itself") is always so much more appealing than sound advice ("Worry about everything")." (*Saturday Review* (January 1986), 36).

I wonder if suspicion of advice is more a characteristic of my generation than yours. Perhaps, when we were your age, back in the long gone 1960s, we just got bad advice. Some random person told me to buy a used car. I did. It died. Somebody else, who told me (at a party my junior year of high school) that he was an expert on technical matters, told me that my life would be great if I bought his old eight-track tape player. "That tape player will last forever," he said. That you have never even seen or heard an eight-track tape in your whole life ought to tell you something about the value of this "expert" advice.

Curiously, many parents today are short on advice. Messers Copenhaver and Robinson have filled these pages with wise counsel. But many parents today are reluctant to tell their children anything. It isn't that your parents don't love you; it's just that many of them are convinced that the future is so strange, that the world you live in is so totally different from where they grew up, that they are loathe to tell you much for fear that they will steer you in the wrong direction. Twenty years later, they fear you'll return saying, "I gave your advice a try and I had a bad life." They never want to be called lousy parents so, even when asked, they tend to be evasive.

The safest way for the cautious parent, when asked, "Mom, what do you think I ought to do with my life?" is to say, "Whatever would make you happy, dear." Trouble is, since you have only lived on this earth for fourteen or maybe sixteen years, how would you know what would make you happy?

There was a time, many years ago, when parents loved to dole out advice. In Shakespeare's Hamlet, young Laertes is on his way out the door for a long road trip. His dad, poor old Polonius, keeps him there forever, droning on: "This above all: to thine own self be true, and it must follow, as the night the day, thou canst not then be false to any man. . . ." What self-respecting parent would risk that today?

Today, about the best that most parents can muster are gems of wisdom like, "Pick up your socks—or you'll never get married," or "Take precautions when dating," hardly the inspiring phrase that you could carve in granite over the door of the library.

We live in the age of post-advice. Advice died my senior year when Dustin Hoffman appeared in *The Graduate*. Ever heard of that movie? It was big when I was about your age. Just after beginning a totally inappropriate relationship with his girlfriend's mother, the recent college graduate is given this advice by the girl's father, who takes him aside and solemnly whispers in his ear, "Plastics."

"Sir?"

"Plastics. Go into plastics."

That, we decided, was the best our parent's generation—pre–civil rights, pre–Vietnam—could give us. *The Graduate* assured my generation that our parents—represented by the "advice" of that father and the lust of that mother—were even more clueless than we and therefore could not be trusted. And so we pledged never to give advice to our kids once we grew up and had kids of our own.

Parental advice in the present age is best characterized by the way Steve Martin ended one of his monologues:

"I have a saying," says Martin, "which I always like to leave with an audience at the end of my show. Something my grandmother told me, which, for me, sums up the meaning of life. And now I would like to share it with you. My grandmother said, 'Son, always . . .' wait, or was it 'Never . . .'?"

And here we come to one of the most amazing characteristics of your generation: You will actually sit still for advice. Maybe you even yearn for advice.

Walking across the Duke University campus one afternoon with a sophomore, listening as he told me about a problem in his life, I was stunned when he turned to me and said, "Well, what do you think I ought to do?"

I could hardly speak. I would have never lowered myself to ask an old codger for advice when I was nineteen! But there he was, asking me, "What do you think?"

Perhaps the world has become so strange, the path to the good life so indistinct that you are among the first generation of young people in a while to be open to, even eager for, advice.

Sitting on a faculty panel discussion one evening in a dormitory before a group of Duke students, I heard a freshman blurt out in exasperation, "Where are you people keeping the stuff? Hand it over! Tell us what you know!"

Tell us what you know. It is an earnest plea from the younger generation to the older. In fact, this may be the main thing that we owe you—to tell you what we know. Oh, I'll tell you that I am reluctant to give you advice because I respect your individuality, that I don't want to force my will on you. Sad to say, what's often meant is, "Kid, stay out of my life and I'll stay out of yours." Don't require me to testify to what I know for fear that you will come back later to correct my errors of judgment. It takes more courage to give advice than youth knows.

In this book, you will encounter two adults—parents, pastors—telling you what they know, in a way that you can hear and understand. Here you will read things that are hard for your parents to talk about with you, things like God and prayer, sex and truth, that are hard for anybody to talk with anybody else about, for that matter. Your life will be better because of this book. My advice to you is, read it, think about it, enjoy it, and then have fun trying to live it.

And don't expect to remember any of this unless you write it down. Get out your felt tips now and start underlining stuff. When you get to be my age you will find that, the older you get, the further away from these youthful years, the less you will remember, even by next week. Write it down or you may not remember.

Remember what?

WILLIAM H. WILLIMON
Dean of the Chapel
Duke University
Durham, North Carolina

Introduction

Dear Laura,

It's been ten years since we started work on this book, *Words for the Journey*, and eight years since it was published. It's a happy surprise that the publisher, The Pilgrim Press, wants to do a new, revised edition. I think that means it's a success.

A lot has happened in the intervening decade in your life and mine, in our family, and in the world: we have our first African-American President; we have Twitter and Facebook; we have Smartphones; and we have the Great Recession. Dictators have been toppled by fed-up people. The climate has grown warmer.

You've graduated from high school and college. You've traveled in Africa and Australia. You're living in your own place and have a job. Both your older brothers are now married. One has children of his own. Three of your grandparents have died in these years, and we miss them a lot.

There's more of course, though that's plenty enough. It strikes me that there's one other experience we've both had some of in these ten years: rejection. Since I see we didn't include any letters on "rejection" or "failure" in the first go-round, I thought I might say a few words on these kinds of experiences, which are some of the harder parts of life.

Let me start by sharing this, which I don't think you know. The first publisher that Martin and I sent this book to turned it down. They rejected it. They did so very politely. Still, the answer was "No." So we tried again. The Pilgrim Press accepted it and published it. It has done well enough for them that they're now doing a new edition.

Maybe there are a few lessons here. First, of course, rejection does happen. Disappointment happens. I can't imagine that anyone gets through life without some such experiences. Some people, however, seem to get far too much of such experiences.

Rejection happens. Disappointment comes our way. We apply for jobs that we don't get. You've discovered that. There are jobs I've applied for in these ten years I didn't get. Sometimes, perhaps even more painfully, rejection happens in relationships. I suspect you know something of that as well. Sometimes you have been the one to end a relationship, to decline the attention and interest of another. That's hard too.

Without trying to stick a smiley face on all such difficult experiences, I would say that, in hindsight, at least some rejections appear to be for the best. This book, for example, probably wasn't the best fit for the first publisher we tried. I think that's pretty true of at least one job I applied for and didn't get—it probably wasn't the right fit, not the right match.

Still, rejection, even if in the long run for the best, isn't much fun in the short run. It knocks the wind out of your sails for a time. It can take a while before you're ready to pick yourself up and go again. But as you've looked for jobs and encountered some rejections, you've done that. You've picked yourself up and tried again. I'm proud of you.

I think such experience is actually really valuable. As life goes on, we can look back and see that there have been hard times and we've come through them, even grown because of them. That strengthens us and gives us perspective when we face new hard times.

Well, you know that I'm going to get around to God and faith stuff eventually. Here it comes. For me "the grace of God" means, at least in part, that life's disappointments, rejections, and failures are never the last word. Our God doesn't give up. Martin likes to say, "Our God insists on having the last word."

From experience, I can testify, there are new beginnings. Always. Sometimes they are a while in coming. But they do come. Grace happens. Sometimes we can't imagine there will be fresh starts, second chances, or new life, but there are.

For a long time, I've kept close some words that sort of express this, at least for me, from Ralph Waldo Emerson:

"Finish every day and be done with it.

Tomorrow is a new day;

You will begin it well and serenely and with too high a spirit

to be cumbered with your old nonsense."

By the grace of God, there are always new beginnings. Know that. Remember it. Trust it. Hold onto it.

Love you forever. Dad

Letters about God

1 · God

Dear Laura,

A not-too-long letter about God. That's a tough assignment!

But in a way you have an even tougher one. I would call it "getting God in the picture." On this score, I think I had it easier than you do. When I was growing up, God was more in the picture than seems to be true today.

What do I mean by that? When I was your age, there were more frequent positive references to God, for one thing, and more agreement about what was meant by the word "God," for another. For instance, most everyone I knew went to church, either a Catholic or Protestant church. A smaller number were Jewish and went to their synagogue. Boy Scouts, a big thing when I was growing up, had a strong religious emphasis. One of the Boy Scout awards was the "God and Country Award." And it was when I was a child that the words "under God" were added to United States Pledge of Allegiance.

Today it's different. For one thing, there are many more people in the United States today who practice religions other than Christianity—Buddhism, Islam, Hinduism, Judaism, to name a few of the major ones. At the very least, that means that there is not as much common understanding or agreement when we speak of God. But maybe even more important than that is another change. Belief in human power and human potential is so great in our society that people often feel no need for God.

Of course, believing in yourself is important, but like all good things, it can be pushed too far. These days, human power, especially through technology, is so great that instead of being content to be human beings, who have limits to their knowledge and their power and their goodness, people end up playing God. People fool themselves into believing that they are in control or in charge of life. Whether it's an individual doing this or a society or government, when human beings play God, when we believe we know it all or can understand everything, it always ends, sooner or later, in disaster.

While different religions understand and describe God in different ways, most all of them agree that human beings are finite, or limited. We see, but not forever. We know, but not fully. We love, but never perfectly. God, on the other hand, is infinite or unlimited, all-seeing, all-knowing, and all-loving. At least part of what it means to say, "I believe in God," is the flip side, "neither I nor any other human being nor any group of human beings is God." The job's already taken. We have our work cut out for us being human.

The primary way that Christians and the church have tried to describe God has been with the doctrine (a word which means teaching, or principle, or set of principles) of the Trinity. The Trinity is not an easy concept to grasp, but that may be part of the point of it. If God is God, then we can never completely understand, or grasp, God.

Still, we need ways to talk about God, ways that do some sort of justice to the ways that people have experienced God. The Trinity helps Christians to talk about how they have experienced God, without letting us imagine that we have God all figured out. In one set of words, the Trinity is "God the Father, the Son, and the Holy Spirit." In another, it is God "the Creator, the Redeemer, and the Sustainer." While not everyone would agree, I don't think the particular names matter as much as what they point to.

One way I think of the Trinity, of what the words point to, is this: God is like water, but is experienced in three different ways. God, who is the Creator of everything that is, is like the hidden groundwater that flows ceaselessly in places beneath the surface of the earth. All life on earth depends on that groundwater, but we can't see it or control it. It is vast, hidden, beyond our knowing, and the source of all that is. God, the first person of the Trinity, is like that.

But God is not only like that. God is also like a spring where the water bubbles up out of the ground and becomes visible. God, the Son or

Redeemer, the second person of the Trinity, is God who becomes visible at a particular point, in a particular life, the life of Jesus of Nazareth. God and God's ways can be known. God is revealed, like a spring reveals the groundwater. In Jesus we see what the invisible and hidden God is like.

But if God, like a spring, bubbles up at a certain place and in a particular life, God is not stuck there. God is also like a stream or a river, flowing from the spring and out to us wherever we are. God, the Spirit or Sustainer, the third person of the Trinity, is like a stream or river, which flows to all sorts of people in every place and time.

It's all the same water—groundwater, spring, and stream—but known in different ways. The doctrine, or teaching, of the Trinity says Christians believe the same God is revealed in three different ways, as Creator, as Christ, as Spirit. In some ways, God is hidden and mysterious like groundwater. In other ways, God is revealed and knowable, in the life and teachings and death and resurrection of Jesus. But if God is revealed in a particular time and place, God is not limited to a certain time and place. Like the river, God comes to every time and place. As I said, the Trinity is not an easy idea, but that's part of what I like about it. I get nervous when God is too easy, or when people think they have God completely figured out.

Besides, what matters most are not our ideas *about* God, but *trust in* God. A prayer that I especially love, written by a great teacher of the church, Martin Luther, points to this truth.

"Eternal God, you call us to ventures of which we cannot see the ending, by paths as yet untrodden, through perils unknown. Give us faith to go out with courage, not knowing where we go, but only that your hand is leading us, and your love supporting us; through Jesus Christ our Lord. Amen."

Love, Dad

2 · Jesus

DEAR TODD,

When you were in sixth grade you were asked to write an essay nominating someone as the "brightest light" of history. You chose Jesus. I must admit that I was a bit surprised by your choice, but I was also delighted. And you did a great job with that essay. I kept a copy of your final draft, but I particularly treasure the first draft you wrote, which I also saved. You wrote that first draft rather quickly, and in one sitting, so it reads differently, as if the words on the page have just sprung fresh from your heart. I hope I can do as good a job in this letter because I want to tell you why Jesus is my "brightest light" as well.

It is difficult to summarize all that Jesus means to me, because he has come to mean so much. For one, Jesus helps me approach God. Without Jesus, God can seem like a rather vague notion, what I once heard someone refer to as a "sacred blur." Or God can seem distant from the kind of life I live, like a monarch who occasionally waves to us from a distant tower. When I recognize God in Jesus, however, the sacred blur is brought into startling focus and God becomes both close and real to me.

I remember a mother telling me about tucking in her young daughter who was afraid to be left alone at bedtime. The mother tried to comfort her by saying that she would remain in the next room and, when that failed to reassure her daughter, the mother told her that God would stay at her bedside and watch over her. But that was not enough, either. The young daughter said, "That's not going to help, Mommy. I need someone with a skin face!" Exactly! And that is not a bad description of what Jesus is: God with a skin face. Sometimes I identify with that little girl more than you might imagine. When I am having difficulty praying, usually it is because God seems too distant or vague. So I talk to Jesus, the God with a skin face, and simply tell him what is on my mind. It makes all the difference.

As you may remember, one of the titles given to Jesus in the Bible is "Emmanuel," which means "God with us." That title is itself a powerful affirmation that has come to mean a great deal to me. It reminds me that, in Jesus, nothing in human life is distant from God. The "skin face" is not like a mask that it is worn lightly and can be taken off if things ever get a bit rough. No, Jesus is human to the bone, which means that he can experience bone-deep sorrow and the kind of joy that can spring from someplace deep as well. In other words, in Jesus, God shares in the kind of life you and I live. So nothing I experience is strange to God. In Jesus, God has been there. And God is there with me. I have drawn strength from that understanding many times over the years, particularly in the hard times, because it helps me know that I am not alone.

Jesus shows me what God is like. Gratefully, I don't have to be a learned philosopher or great saint to grasp what God is like, because I am neither. All I have to do is look at Jesus. God is Jesus-like. We learn about God not only from Jesus' teachings, but also from his life. He tells us and he shows us. And we learn some surprising things, things we might not have guessed or known without Jesus. For instance, with the way our world is ordered we wouldn't necessarily know that God has special affection for the last, the least, and the lost. Jesus told his followers this, but he also demonstrated it by seeking out those whom the world rejects. Jesus said that we should forgive our enemies, which is just what he did when his enemies hung him on the cross. When he was about to die, Jesus told his followers that God is more powerful than evil or death. They probably struggled to picture what that might mean and, even if they could picture it, I'm sure it was difficult for them to believe. But then came Easter, to show the lengths to which God will go to offer life and love. In these and other ways we learn not only what Jesus is like, but also what God is like. From Jesus we learn that God is more compassionate, forgiving, and powerful than we might otherwise have known or dared believe.

Jesus not only shows us what God is like, but also what we can be. He reveals not only what God is like, but also what it is to be fully human. In all complex tasks we need someone to show us how it's done. When you wanted to learn how to play squash, you read several books. After you had finished those books you knew a lot about the game. You understood the rules and you even knew something about the technique. But no one can learn how to play squash by reading a book! You didn't learn how to play the game until you started taking lessons from someone who could show you how it's done. It's like that with complex tasks. There are certain things that can't be learned from books. Rules and instructions aren't enough. Someone has to show you how it's done. If that is true of something like squash, how much more is that the case with learning how to live a full and faithful human life? Jesus shows us how it's done.

I'm sure you have seen the letters "WWJD" on bumper stickers and jewelry, and you probably know that they stand for, "What would Jesus do?" It has been something of a fad, so I'm sure that not all those who wear the jewelry have given much thought to the implications, much less tried to let the question guide their lives. But it is a great question to ask. It is simple, some would say too much so, but I think that is part of its value. When I am faced with challenging people, difficult decisions, or competing demands, it is amazing how often that simple question can bring clarity. Sometimes the answer is not immediately obvious. It can be hard to know just what Jesus might do in some circumstances. More often, however, the answer is all too obvious and I just may not want to hear it!

Ultimately, however, I love Jesus not because he can help me to be a better person, but because he brings God's love to me even when I am not a better person. Jesus is so much more than God's human self-improvement plan. And that's a good thing, too, because even with his teachings and example, I would surely blow it. If it were left to me, I would find a way to mess up. So Jesus is not our way to reach God as much as God's way to reach out to us.

That's why Easter is such an important event for Christians. When we did our worst, God did God's best, responding to our hate with love, answering our violence with forgiveness, taking death and trumping it with new life. Easter means, as the Apostle Paul put it, "Nothing in all creation can separate us from the love of God in Christ Jesus our Lord." Nothing that we do, nothing that we fail to do, nothing within us or outside us, nothing we know or imagine, no person, no force, no thing, *nothing* can come between us and the God who loves us, the God we are invited to know in Jesus Christ.

That is why Jesus is the brightest light in my life and in the life of the world. Or, as you said when you concluded your essay, "He is the brightest light of them all, even more than the North Star." You were so right, Todd. As your life unfolds and your relationship with Jesus grows, I don't think you will need to add anything to that statement except, "Amen" and "Amen."

LOVE, D.

3 · Holy Spirit

DEAR TODD,

I don't remember there being much talk about the Holy Spirit in my home church when I was growing up. It was almost as if there was, "The Father, the Son, . . . and that other guy." I have come to see that as a real loss because I have since come not only to understand more about the Holy Spirit, but also to rely on the Holy Spirit and to delight in the Spirit's presence. So I want to make sure you get to know the Holy Spirit early on. Consider this your letter of introduction.

The Bible introduces us to the Holy Spirit early and often, but that may be part of the problem. Each time the Spirit is described, it can be in such a new way that we may be tempted to ask, "Excuse me, but have we met before?" But there is one image that is used more than any other, an image that is contained in a single word that can be translated as "breath," "wind," and "spirit."

The interplay of those different dimensions, all contained in the word used in the Bible for Holy Spirit, is very revealing. It reminds me that the continuing presence of the Holy Spirit is necessary for life to be sustained. If the Spirit were removed, we creatures would surely perish, as surely as if breath were removed. The Holy Spirit can be as gentle as breath on a mirror or as awesome as a hurricane that lifts a house from its foundations. We cannot see the Holy Spirit, but we can know when the Spirit is present, just as we cannot see the wind, but we do not question its presence when it slaps our cheeks in January or embraces us with warmth in May. We do not see the wind, but we can see the way it rustles through the leaves of a tree. We know the Spirit is present because we see what the Spirit does.

What is perhaps most surprising is that we can see the Holy Spirit at work through us. The Holy Spirit can be within us, and flow through us, like breath. One of the most helpful descriptions I have heard of the Holy Spirit is "the God who comes up through us." That is, it is through the Holy Spirit that the power and love of God can be at work through us, even through people like us. The Holy Spirit can billow through us in ways that can make us stronger, surer, more faithful, more capable, than we might otherwise be.

There are certain times when I am reminded that something beyond me can be at work in my life. For instance, there are those occasions when I get into the pulpit to preach a sermon with an unmistakable sense of dread. The sermon just hasn't come together. I have wrestled with it all week and, clearly, I have lost the match. My words don't come close to expressing what I want to say. I want to begin with an apology, but I remember that when I was learning to preach I was told that one should never do that. So I give it my best shot. After worship I would rather slink away, embarrassed by my feeble effort. But then someone will say to me, "How did you know that that is just what I needed to hear today?" I didn't, of course. The feeble sermon was mine; the power came from somewhere else.

Or I will go into a hospital room of someone who is very ill. I mostly just listen and express care with a few words, which seems so inadequate under the circumstances. Before I leave, I offer a prayer, perhaps fearful that even the words of my prayer are too weak and heavy to find their way to God. In those circumstances, sometimes I wish that I were a doctor or nurse, someone who could actually do something to help. Then, perhaps some time later, I might hear from the patient, or her family, that my visit made all the difference. Something in my prayer, or in just my presence, was encouraging and comforting, healing even. It is always humbling to hear of such things because it means that, in ways I cannot account for, something powerful occurred in that room that was not of my doing, yet somehow worked through me. We can speak of these things as we might speak of a mystery. And they are a mystery, but this mystery has a name: the Holy Spirit.

Perhaps you have experienced this in another realm. Your jazz band teacher told your mother and me that he is quite astounded by your ability on the bass guitar. He knows that you haven't had many lessons and that you don't practice very often. So how is it that you are able to come up with such sophisticated bass riffs? He is at a loss to explain it. But I see it as your special gift, a gift of the Holy Spirit.

Creative people often confess that the source of their special gifts is a mystery even to them. The great operatic tenor, Luciano Pavorotti, attests to this same mystery by referring to his own voice in the third person, as if it comes from another source that is beyond him. It is through the Holy Spirit that God invites us to share in the joy of creation. In fact, the Hebrew word for Spirit of God and the word for artistic skill can be used synonymously. The Spirit of God is a creative spirit, which not only created the world once, but continues to create, even through us.

The Holy Spirit works in each life differently, not just through artistic skill, but also through the full range of gifts. The gifts may differ, but it is the same Holy Spirit at work through each one.

Perhaps now you can understand why I thought of the Holy Spirit when we saw the *Star Wars* movies. In those movies people were trained in how to call upon "the Force," a mysterious power that can do great and mighty things through otherwise very ordinary people. The Holy Spirit is something like that, except that, unlike "the Force," the Holy Spirit is not an impersonal power but a personal presence. The Holy Spirit is a "you" and not an "it." That means that instead of asking, "What is the Holy Spirit?" we ask, "Who is the Holy Spirit?" And this is the answer: It is the same God who created the heavens and the earth, the same God who came to us in Jesus Christ, who is now at work through us and among us.

Even as the Holy Spirit can work within us and through us, like breath, that same Spirit can be between us and among us, like air. The Holy Spirit is not only God within us, but also God between us. In fact, the Spirit's true home is community.

It is because the Holy Spirit is known in different ways in each life that we gather in community. No one can boast of having all the spiritual gifts. No one individual can have all the gifts offered by the Spirit, but when we are in community, the gifts that are given to others can bless us as well. So, for instance, your gift of music, as a gift from the Spirit, is given to you not just for your own enjoyment, but also for the benefit of others who do not have that same gift.

If the Holy Spirit requires community to be fully manifest, the same Spirit offers what it requires. It is through the Spirit that we can gather with people we did not choose and be bound to them in ways that are as firm as they are mysterious. Although the Spirit may be at work in various communities, the church is the community in which the Holy Spirit is called upon as the source of the community's life. It is in the church that the mysterious force at work in so much of life is called upon by its proper name: Holy Spirit. May *that* force be with you. May the Holy Spirit, the delightful presence of God I already see at work in you in so many ways, continue to fill your life as the wind fills a sail.

Love, D.

4 · Faith

DEAR LAURA,

What is faith?

I think of Noah, hammering away on planks of gopher wood and building his ark, while his neighbors snorted into their beards and laughed to themselves about "crazy Noah."

What is faith?

I think of Abraham and Sarah who set out from their home. They left behind family, possessions, and everything else they knew. They set out for what they didn't know.

What is faith?

I think of Moses going, against his better judgment, to get in the face of the most powerful political leader of the day and say, "Let my people go."

What is faith?

I think of Mary, a young, peasant girl, with life in her womb and a song on her lips. "My soul magnifies the Lord," she sang, "for God has brought down the mighty and lifted up the lowly."

What is faith?

I think of the unnamed woman in the Gospels whose bleeding problem got her labeled "impure" and sentenced to isolation. Despite that she risked going out in public, going into a crowd so that she could touch Jesus.

What is faith?

I think of Paul, Jewish through and through, heading off into the strange forbidden world of the Gentiles, and in doing so walking straight through walls of perception and prejudice a good deal more solid than sheet rock.

When trying to say what faith is the author of the Letter to the Hebrews does offer a definition. "Faith is the assurance of things hoped for, the conviction of things not seen." (Heb. 11:1). But mostly whoever wrote that letter cites examples and tells stories. "There was this one, and that one. And oh, that reminds me of . . ." On and on (see chapter 11 of the Letter to the Hebrews) until he says, "Enough already! You get the idea."

Do we get the idea? What is the idea of faith? It has something to do with answering, with responding, with saying "yes" to something or someone that is usually not nearly so plain as the nose on your face. Every one of the people whose names I have mentioned, whose stories I have alluded to here, was responding to some intrusion into his or her life, some disruptive word, some unexpected calling, some wild love.

Noah, for example, didn't just take a notion to build a really big boat. He somehow heard a word, a command. Neither did Abraham and Sarah simply feel a yen for travel. Something broke into their settled lives and said, "Leave it all behind. Go to a land I will show you."

Moses had no intention at all of leading a political uprising or an Exodus of the Hebrew slaves from Egypt. But then he found that the old familiar ground where he was herding his sheep was suddenly ground so holy he had to remove his sandals and stand barefoot, and listen to a strange voice speaking from a flaming bush, a voice that called his name.

On and on. Mary was minding her own business when a winged messenger showed up to announce that she was to be a mother of God. Paul was intent on his religious duties, which at the time mostly consisted of rounding up and torturing Christians, when a light shone so brightly in his eyes that he went temporarily blind and a voice drove him to his knees. (I guess some people have a harder time paying attention than others!)

Faith is a way of responding to these unexpected intrusions, to these words we have not spoken but heard, to directions we have neither given nor invented, but received. Faith is Abraham and Sarah, to be sure not without apprehensions, setting out on a journey anyhow. Faith is Moses trusting, against all the political pundits and polls of the time, that God meant business when he said, "Let my people go!" Faith is Mary saying, "Let it be," when she might just as well have pretended that the angel Gabriel was the result of a fit of indigestion and then gone back to her knitting. Faith has everything to do with risk and trust.

That's why the opposite of faith is not doubt. I am pretty sure that every one of the people whose names I've mentioned had their doubts. No, the opposite of faith is not doubt. It is fear.

It is fear that keeps us stuck on the sidelines of life. It is fear that traps our voices inside our throats. It is fear that paralyzes our limbs and keeps us from standing up and setting out when the thing we most need to do is move. To say that the opposite of faith is fear is not to say that Abraham and Sarah, Moses and Mary, never experienced fear. I am sure they did. What they did not do was give fear the trump card or the final vote. They did not let their fear shut them down.

The apostle Paul says that faith is a gift, not our achievement. Maybe that is because faith is always the second word. The first word is God's. "Go." "Come." "Listen." "Speak." "Follow me." These are God's words to us. They come first. They come unbidden, as gift (see my letter on "Grace"). The second word is ours. "Let's pack." "Okay." "Yes." "If you say so." But maybe even the capacity to respond in trust is a gift. Faith is, for sure, not our achievement. It is God's work in us.

In the Gospel of John faith in Christ is described as the difference between life and death. John isn't just talking about what happens to us after we die. He means here and now. To be caught up in faith, to answer with all we have and all we are, to risk everything on the crazy notion that love is stronger than death and that God is at work in the world, is to be alive. If we don't answer, if we just pretend it was nothing, we will probably go on living, only not really.

Some years ago, before I went to seminary or became a minister, your mother and I were living in Hawaii on the Big Island. I was teaching at a community college, and your mother was driving a school bus. When we discovered that she was pregnant with our first child, your brother, Joe, I took a second job, working as a janitor at night cleaning hotels.

One night I was working alone vacuuming a large, glass-walled hotel ballroom, next to the ocean, when an earthquake began to shake everything. The tables and chairs, the doors and the glass walls all trembled and rolled. Then, as quickly as it had begun, it ended. The stillness that followed seemed eerie. Somehow in the silence a question was framed to me and for me. It was "Are you going to live out of your hope or your fear?" It was a faith question, maybe the faith question. Ever since it was asked in the stillness that followed that earthquake, I have remembered it. I have tried to live, more nearly, from my hope and my faith, than from my fears. I have tried to live, that is, in and by trust. For in the end, faith more than anything else means trust.

LOVE, DAD

5 · Doubt

DEAR TODD,

For as long as I can remember I have been interested in the subject of doubt. Perhaps that's because I have known so many people who have struggled with doubt, and probably also because I recognize that I am one of them. We sometimes speak as if there are two kinds of people: those who believe in God and those who do not. But such clear distinctions are only rarely reflected in the lives of real people. I have known many people of deep faith, whose entire lives are shaped by their relationship with God, and yet doubt still visits them, on occasion at least. I have also known people who contend that they have rejected the very idea that there is a God, and yet they also have moments when they doubt their doubts. A man who came to Jesus seeking help probably speaks for most of us when he said, "I believe; help my unbelief."

I have concluded that doubt is not always the enemy of faith, and sometimes can actually help our relationship with God grow. To be sure, doubt can be unsettling, even painful in its own way—but then, those things that prompt us to grow are often like that, aren't they?

Doubt can help us grow in our faith when it causes us to move beyond inadequate ideas of God. For instance, I wonder what would have happened if I never doubted the beliefs of my childhood. Whatever beliefs first occupied my mind would have taken up permanent residence. I would still think of my parents as all-powerful and myself as immortal. I would still believe that my parents could take me to the Land of Oz on the next family vacation. I would still picture God living behind a cloud, picnicking with my deceased grandparents and getting crumbs in his beard. Somewhere along the line I had to doubt all of these ideas to make room for other beliefs.

When people say to me that they do not believe in God, often I ask in response, "What is the God that you do not believe in?" Often the God they describe is small and simplistic. They don't believe in a God who is like a kindly grandfather. Or, by contrast, they don't believe in a God who is a cruel snatcher of souls, visiting death upon children because "he wants them with him in heaven." To such descriptions of God I can only respond, "I don't believe in that God either." Sometimes our doubts are a way to reject inadequate images of God.

There is another way in which doubt can help us deepen our faith. When we are young children, usually we accept without question the religious beliefs of our parents. It is a secondhand faith. There is nothing wrong with that, of course. Such inherited faith is a way to grow in one's own faith by trying on the beliefs and practices of those who are older. But when a child becomes a young adult something quite different can happen. Those same religious beliefs can be rejected because they are held by the same parents! This change of attitude is not necessarily a bad thing, either. Often it is necessary to disengage from our inherited beliefs so that, at a later stage, we may come to believe again, but with a big difference. The beliefs are now our own. They are not someone else's hand-me-downs. For an adult, particularly a young adult, a time of doubt can be as important as activating the clutch of a car: It allows you to shift from a secondhand faith to a firsthand faith.

I don't mean to imply that doubt is something that we will merely grow out of in time. I have been struck by the ways in which the towering figures in Christian history confessed to their doubts, even as they testified to their faith. I think we could draw some rather meager lessons from the presence of doubt in the lives of these great believers. We might simply conclude that no one is perfect. Or we might cite doubt as evidence that belief is simply too difficult to sustain. But something more seems to be at work here. We sometimes speak of doubt and faith as opposites, but perhaps it is more accurate to think of doubt as the shadow cast by faith. Where there is little faith, there is less potential for doubt. Where faith is towering, the shadow of doubt can be that much greater.

It seems to me that a God who is worthy of belief will always be subject to doubt. After all, the only things we do not doubt are things like 2 + 2 = 4. But who would worship a 2 + 2 = 4 kind of God? A God who could be so easily understood would lack depth and mystery, and all the dimensions of personality. Rather, such a God would be predictable, easy to understand. And if God were that predictable and that easy to understand, we might eliminate doubt, but we would also eliminate the grandeur and majesty of God. As a wise person once said, "A God you could understand would be less than yourself."

In other words, the only way to eliminate all doubt is to reduce God to something that is unworthy of our devotion. Only a God who is too mighty to be encompassed by certainty, too wonderful to be found only within the borders of our imaginations, is worthy of such devotion. In other words, only a God we could doubt is worth believing in!

So I am not concerned if you have doubts about God along the way. Sometimes doubt plays an important role in the life of faith. If you encounter doubt, however—as you almost surely will—I would have these hopes for you:

First, I hope that you will feel free to express your doubts. I say this not only because doubts are nothing to be ashamed of, but also because I have learned that doubts are like mushrooms—they grow best in the dark. Expressing doubts has a way of diminishing their power.

Second, I hope that you will not conclude that any doubts you might have disqualify you from a life of faith. Believe in as much God as you can. Work from whatever corner of belief you have. Any of us could spend our lives focused on the doubts we have, but most of us have enough beliefs to keep us busy for a lifetime.

Finally, I hope that you will be patient with those things that you cannot yet understand or accept. I once heard about a famous preacher who had three file drawers. One was labeled, "Accepted," and in it he put slips of paper on which he had written those things that he firmly believed. Another file was labeled, "Rejected." That was for all the things he simply could not accept. But the third file was the largest. It was labeled, "Awaiting Further Light." I hope you will have such a file in your own heart and mind. The presence of such a file demonstrates an openness to new understanding. It says that you don't have all the answers yet and don't need to. Put in it all those things about which you are not yet certain. Use it for all of those things people you trust have told you, but you have not yet accepted for yourself. Fill it with those affirmations you might put in the "Rejected" file were it not for the accumulated witness of the Christian tradition saying, "You may not fully believe this now, but please trust us enough to put it somewhere where you will be sure to consider it again."

In all of this my prayer is not that your life will be free from doubt, for that may not be possible. Rather, my prayer is that any doubt in your life will be like the shadow that reflects the height and depth of your faith.

LOVE, D.

6 · Suffering

Dear Todd,

I want to write to you about what I consider the greatest challenge to faith in God—the existence of suffering. Why does God allow innocent people to be stricken with terrible diseases? And why do so many prayers for healing seem not to be answered? Why does God permit war? Why doesn't God stand in the way of a hurricane that is about to mow down houses and destroy lives? Suffering prompts many questions. I wish I could answer those questions, but I cannot. I know, even as I begin this letter, that I will not be able to explain suffering. Many of the greatest minds of history have tried and none have succeeded. Why innocent people suffer is a stubborn mystery.

It isn't difficult to summarize why suffering is such a challenge to faith. Christians believe both that God is all-loving and that God is all-powerful. But how does one square those two realities with the third reality that terrible things happen? Logically, we could affirm any two of those realities without much difficulty. For instance, we could imagine an all-loving God who was powerless to stop terrible things from happening. Or, we could imagine an all-powerful God who was not loving enough to stop terrible things from happening. But Christians have always affirmed that God is both all-loving and all-powerful.

We could imagine a God who is so loving and so powerful that nothing bad ever happens. But that would be counter to our experience in the world, where suffering is an everyday reality. What can seem difficult—if not impossible—to affirm are all three realities: God is all-loving; God is all-powerful; terrible things happen.

That's why suffering is such a challenge to faith. And it's not just a puzzle to ponder at a distance. It hits home and it hits hard as we see innocent people suffer or experience suffering ourselves.

Many adults, when they encounter someone who lives with some great grief or sorrow, try to explain suffering. Often these explanations are attempts to find meaning in suffering. They offer reasons why something has happened. In response to someone's crushing loss or hardship, they might say something like, "Perhaps this was given to you as an opportunity to grow." Or, "This must be part of God's plan." One response that I commonly hear in the face of death is, "God must have wanted her with him." Usually I get the impression that when people say such things they don't really mean what they say. They just don't know *what* to say. So they try one thing, and then another, like a doctor who knows of no cure so, in desperation, tries whatever medicine is close at hand. But, try as we might, such attempts at explanation never really work. To offer explanations in response to suffering is to say more than we know.

You may remember hearing about the man named Job, whose story is told in the Bible. Just about everything that could go wrong in his life did go wrong, terribly wrong. One day he was the richest man around, and the next day he was wiped out. His entire flock of sheep was destroyed in a fire when lightning hit his sheep barn. His seven children were killed when a hurricane crushed the house where they were staying. Then Job himself got sick and was covered with painful sores.

When Job's friends came to pay a call on him, they each offered a theory about why this had happened to him. One theorized that his suffering was a way of purifying his soul. Another thought it must be some form of punishment. A third said it must be a test of Job's faith. All of them made the common mistake of thinking that what Job needed from them was an explanation for his suffering. God is also a character in the story of Job. But, unlike Job's friends, God does not explain Job's suffering. In fact, God is the only one who doesn't even try to explain.

In contrast to the well-meaning folk who try to give reasons why people suffer, the Bible in general doesn't offer much in the way of explanations.

The mystery of suffering is not solved. What the Bible does offer, however, are affirmations that God helps those who suffer. God comforts, strengthens, and upholds those who suffer. Those who suffer are especially dear to God. The most powerful way in which God helps those who suffer is by sharing their suffering.

That is one reason why Christians view the cross as so central to our faith. It is on the cross, in the willingness of Jesus to suffer and die, that God takes on the kind of life we live. Our God is not a distant figure. We worship a God who suffers and chooses to be with us in our suffering. I remember someone telling me about picking up his daughter at kindergarten. She was late in coming out of the classroom and looked upset when she finally emerged. She explained to her father that her friend had just broken a ceramic dish he had been working on and planned to give to his parents. Her father said, "So you stayed to help him pick up the pieces?" "No," she corrected her father. "I stayed to help him cry." To be sure, sometimes God helps us pick up the pieces in our lives. But other times God simply shares our suffering and helps us cry. That understanding has come to mean a great deal to me.

Last year I went to a concert at Alanna's school. One of the songs the chorus sang was a traditional spiritual, "Nobody Knows the Trouble I Seen." The song is the wrenching cry of a soul who knows what it is to suffer. The old saying is that "misery loves company," but most people who suffer find it a lonely, isolating experience. So the first verse of the song says, "Nobody knows the trouble I seen, Nobody knows my sorrow." I have always been moved by that song, and I was on this occasion. It is so honest and filled with longing. I kept waiting for the final verse, because I felt a great longing myself. That verse is different, and includes the affirmation: "Nobody knows the trouble I seen, Nobody knows but Jesus." It is a statement of faith that, whatever hardship we face, we do not face it alone. Jesus knows because Jesus is with us in our suffering. But they never sang that verse! I suppose they didn't feel able to make such a faith statement at a school concert. So they just ended the song with the expression of lonely, unrelieved suffering ("nobody knows . . . nobody knows"). The song left me with an empty feeling. It reminded me again why I am so grateful that I know one who chooses to suffer with us, who does not leave us alone. It made me very glad that I know Jesus.

And because we face suffering with Jesus at our side, we are able to face it with hope. We know how the story of Jesus ends, not with the suffering of Good Friday, but with the triumph of Easter. Jesus shares our suffering so that we might, in turn, share in his victory. Here is the way I have come to understand this mystery: Our God is the kind of God who insists on having the last word. The second to last word, which can be very powerful, can be given to something else—suffering, despair, hopelessness, disease, even death itself. But our God is the kind of God who insists on having the very last word, and that is always a helpful word and a hopeful word, a word of comfort, of healing, and of life.

To be sure, there are times when we wish we could understand suffering. But in the end we are given something more powerful than an explanation. We are given the assurance that, in Jesus, God shares in our suffering—deeply, intimately, in a way that no one else can. And then we are given the additional assurance that suffering is not the last word. As Easter demonstrates, the story isn't over until we have heard from the God who insists on having the last word. Gratefully, we worship a God who always bats last. Is it any wonder, then, that the Christian story is called "the gospel"—that is, "the good news?"

Love, D.

7 · Sin

Dear Todd,

Recently I had a conversation with someone who objects to our congregation's practice of including a prayer of confession in our worship service. She concluded her remarks by declaring, "I am not a sinner! And I don't come to church to feel badly about myself!" She let it be known that there was nothing more she wanted to say or hear on the subject, although perhaps we will continue that conversation at some point. Likely it will not be a short conversation, however, because we hear the same words in very different ways. Obviously, to her, the word "sin" is as heavy as a millstone; to me, it is a hopeful word. To her, confession feels something like a trip to the vice-principal's office; to me, confession is like being shown the way to freedom after time spent in captivity.

I don't know how the word "sin" sounds to your ears, but I want to explain to you why, to me, it is among the most hopeful, freeing words in the Christian vocabulary.

There are many related definitions of sin, but a good place to start is with the definition of sin as disobeying God. When the woman declared, "I am not a sinner," I think she was trying to make clear that she has not broken any of God's commandments. She hasn't killed anyone. She doesn't steal. She can't think of a time she has lied. She hasn't committed adultery. I can say the same things about myself. At least, I can claim I am innocent if I interpret those commandments in the narrowest possible way.

For instance, I can't think of a time I have stolen anything (at least, not since I used to take quarters off my father's dresser when I was a boy). But Ghandi once said that the surplus bread in your cupboard is stolen from the poor. (Actually, Gramme used to say something very similar. I can still hear her saying, "I think it's a sin to have something you don't use when someone else can use it.") In that sense, I steal things every day.

In a similar way, it would be hard for me to remember the last time I told an out-and-out lie. But sometimes I do say things that are not the entire truth. I think we all tell "social lies" in response to questions like, "Do you like my dress?" Usually such lies are relatively harmless because they are told in order not to hurt someone else's feelings and because little else is at stake. But then we tell other kinds of lies, when more is at stake, such as when we make excuses (for instance, "I didn't get it done because I was sick," when that was only one reason, or, "I was there, but I really didn't have any idea what was going on," when you know more than you let on). We tell these kinds of lies, not to avoid hurting someone else, but to make ourselves look better in other people's eyes. I think we all shade the truth in one way or another all of the time. Your grandfather was once in a play in which the main character was compelled to tell the truth for an entire day. He couldn't do it! As I remember, he was not a very admirable character to begin with, but I think even good people would find it difficult to speak the whole truth for any length of time.

In the Sermon on the Mount, Jesus said that anyone who looks at a woman with lust has already committed adultery in his heart (Matt. 5:28). By using a wider net in his definition of adultery, everyone gets caught. I like the *New Yorker* cartoon featuring a couple leaving church after a sermon that obviously interpreted the Ten Commandments in this broader way. The man turns to his wife and says, "Well, at least I haven't made any graven images lately" (which is one of the Ten Commandments). In other words, the sermon helped him identify the ways in which he had broken the other nine!

I don't think Jesus broadens the conventional definition of sin so that more people will feel guilty; I think he does it so that more people won't feel self-righteous. If adultery is defined only in a narrow way, some of us get to feel self-satisfied, but then Jesus prompts us to examine our own behavior, coaxing the realization that sin has a thousand faces and surely one of them is ours.

In addition to all of the ways we disobey God by the things we say or do, we also must add all the things we should have said or done and did not. We sin not only when we do something that God tells us not to do; we also sin when we don't do something God has asked us to do. It is when we consider those things that we have not done that our list of sins really begins to add up. It includes not just the cruel things I said, but also all the kind words I did not say. I disobey God not just when I steal, but also when I do not help someone who is poor. It is not enough that I haven't killed anyone, because I must also account for all the ways I have failed to work for an end to violence in the world. The list of things I have done may be long, but the list of things I have failed to do is virtually endless.

But still we are not finished. In addition to those things I have done or failed to do as an individual, I am also part of a human race that has disobeyed God in a whole range of complex and intermingled ways. These are called "corporate sins" (in this context "corporate" means body, referring to the larger body of humankind of which we are all a part). So even if, as an individual, you never disobeyed God (you would be the first, by the way, but see my point here), you would not be entirely blameless because your life is so enmeshed in the life of humankind, including its sins.

Corporate sins are so tangled up with human life that we cannot disassociate ourselves from them. For example, even something as seemingly harmless as driving a car is a way to participate in the sins of humankind. After all, the tires of the car may be made with rubber from countries where the workers are kept poor and are forced to work in terrible conditions. The gas that fuels the car is available and cheap because our country has waged war on other countries that threatened our oil supply. Burning gas contributes to pollution of the environment. You may not choose to participate in such conditions, but you do so just by driving a car. If we do all of that just by driving a car, imagine all the ways in which we are involved in other sins of humankind, whether we mean to or not.

Perhaps now you can see why I could not agree with the woman who said, "I am not a sinner." When we survey all the things we have done and failed to do, and then add all of the sins of humankind in which we take part, the list is very long, indeed.

Even such a complete inventory would not tell the whole story, however, because sin is not just a matter of failing to comply with a long list of "do's" and "don'ts." If it were, then it might be enough simply to try harder. But it is not that simple. The ways in which we disobey God are like symptoms of a deeper condition. Not only do we disobey God in particular instances, we also have a deep and stubborn tendency to rebel against God. Because of our rebelliousness, our souls lean toward sin in such a way that even a determined effort to do better is simply not enough. We get caught in destructive cycles. Here is a comparison: You could disobey me often enough that our relationship was in some way broken and in need of repair. Then again, if our relationship were in some way broken, you would probably disobey me all the more.

The only way to break such cycles is through forgiveness. And that is why confession is so important. Through confession we seek more than forgiveness for particular sins. We also seek a restoration of relationships, so that whatever stands between us might be put behind us.

Confession is not dwelling on the negative, any more than a doctor giving an accurate diagnosis can be accused of being negative. Rather, it is the first step in being healed.

As Christians, we look at the people around us and look at ourselves, and we are free to say the truth. We are sinners. Good and bad are inextricably intertwined within us. As the Apostle Paul put it, "All have sinned and fallen short of the glory of God." There can be something wonderfully freeing in simply facing the truth about ourselves. We can do that and not despair because we do not put our trust in ourselves, but in God. Some people may need to believe that they are always lovable, but Christians are free to recognize that we are not lovable because we know that God loves us anyway.

That is why sin is a hopeful word. When we recognize sin we are free to claim God's forgiveness. What was once a chasm becomes a bridge. We don't have to rely on our own goodness anymore. The point of confession is not to feel badly about ourselves. Rather, it is a way to cling to the goodness of God.

And that is why I say that, to me, the word "sin" is among the most hopeful, freeing words in the Christian vocabulary.

Love, D.

8 · Grace

Dear Laura,

When your mother and I were falling in love we happened to spend a day together on the Oregon Coast. As we walked along the beach I carved five letters, each about twelve feet high, into the sand. When I was done it said, "LUCKY," and that's how I felt. Incredibly lucky to be in love, to be loved by the woman who was to become your mother. It was all a gift and I knew it. I didn't deserve this wondrous thing that had happened to me, nor had I managed to bring it about by my ardent and clever courting. It was grace.

Grace means something like this: You are loved not because you are always loveable or deserving or appealing or because you have measured up to some standard, but just because. Because that's the way God is. God loves recklessly. Before our faith in God is God's faith in us. God's faith in us is grace. God's acts on our behalf are grace.

For me grace has been a genuine lifesaver. Through some combination of circumstances I got the notion as I grew up that if I tried hard enough and was good enough, I would be loved by God, the world, my parents, and myself. The catch was that I had to be on my toes at all times, and striving for achievement and perfection. I had to shine brighter and do better than others. There are at least two problems with this. The first is that it is a terrible lot of work. The second is that it doesn't work.

Striving to achieve, to stand out, to be better and smarter than the next person is not only a lot of work, but it's not very happy or enjoyable work.

You can pretty easily end up like the older brother in Jesus' parable of the prodigal son (Luke 15:11–32). When the father in that story not only forgives his younger, prodigal, son, but also makes a fool of himself falling all over his errant child, the older brother is beside himself. He is fuming.

His father's forgiving and joyous welcome of his brother drives him crazy. It's not fair. Here he, the elder brother, has worked himself to a frazzle day after day. He has been the good son who has kept the family farm going, without any help from his no-good brother, thanks very much! Now, after that same brother has blown off a sizeable chunk of the family fortune, their father does not demand that he shape up, or that he work off the debt. Instead, the old man goes running down the road, makes a fool of himself falling all over the boy, and throws a party for him. When the older brother comes in from a hard day's work, he can't believe it. He is furious. He kept the rules and where did it get him!

He is fuming because it's not fair. And he is right. Grace is not fair.

When we believe that everyone should get just what they deserve, no more and no less, and that life should operate on a strict system of fairness and just desserts, grace is offensive.

Grace means that when we deserve a closed door, we find an open one instead. Grace means that when we ought to be tossed in the penalty box, we get a party. Grace means that when we deserve a slap in the face, we get smothered in a hug.

The problem that the older brother in the parable has, the problem that I have struggled with throughout my life, is a human problem. Most all of us, one way or another, struggle with this problem. Most of us imagine we play by the rules and deserve better than we get. We can't stand it when someone who doesn't play by the rules (at least as we see it) is rewarded. But from God's point of view, none of us plays perfectly by the rules. From God's point of view all of us are screw-ups. The older brother was, in his own way, as much a screw-up as the younger brother. Plodding along day after day, he never realized how much his father loved him. He never found any joy in that love or in his work. But the father in that story, and God, loves the older brothers (and sisters) too. Not because they have earned it, but just because.

So here's what it comes down to: Christianity is a religion of grace. It is not a religion of virtue, nor is it a religion of rules. What's the difference? A religion of virtue says, "If you measure up, if you are good enough, if you are truly virtuous, then God will love you." A religion of grace says, "God loves you, therefore, act like it." Grace comes first.

It's this way in story after story in the Bible. The grace of freedom (the Exodus) comes first. Only afterwards are the Hebrew people led to Mount Sinai and given the Ten Commandments (the Law). The Law, in the Bible, is how people who are loved and know it, how people who have experienced saving grace, are to shape their lives and their life together.

It's the same in the New Testament. The grace of resurrection, which brought with it a second chance and forgiveness for Jesus' disciples who had deserted him and denied him when the chips were down, comes first. Only after the disciples are startled and astonished that God has not deserted them, but returned, and that Jesus is in some strange way alive, is the church called into being.

That's the grammar of the Gospel. Grace and response. First comes grace, then our response. (See my letter "What is Faith?")

Wherever and whenever Christians and the church have forgotten this, Christianity has become moralistic and legalistic and joyless. It turns into a religion that is all about keeping the rules, about appearances, about deciding who's in and who's out. It turns into, in other words, a religion that is all about us and our doing, and nothing about God and God's doing. It turns into a religion of good works and achievement and ceases to be a religion of grace. When this happens it is only a matter of time until God breaks in to blow the whole thing sky high.

Several years ago there was an evangelistic campaign that tried to win people to Christianity. The slogan of the campaign was "I Found It!" I guess that meant, I found the truth, or I found God, or I found love. I always thought they had it backwards. I thought the slogan should be "It Found Me!" At least that's the way I've experienced it. Or as John Newton put it in his famous hymn "Amazing Grace," "I once was lost, but now am found, was blind but now I see."

LOVE, DAD

Letters about the Church

9 · The Church

DEAR LAURA,

As you know, I have been the minister at Plymouth Church for over ten years now. At your age ten years probably seems like a very long time! One of the things that is good about being part of a congregation for as long as that (and in some other ways ten years is a very short time) is you see, and are a part of, changes in peoples lives. I love this about the church.

There are some changes that are easy to spot: A child is born. A toddler turns into a teenager. A couple is married. Another couple is divorced. People grow up and grow old. Some take their place in our midst as adults, while others slow down until it's all they can do to simply show up and smile. During ten years' time someone that you have come to love, and whom you can't imagine life or the church without, dies or moves away. And new people enter the congregation's life and become so much a part of it that you can hardly remember what it was like before they were there.

There are other changes that are harder to spot—less visible, but no less real, changes in people's lives. For some, faith deepens and matures. You see people "rise to the occasion," whatever the occasion may be—serving as a leader, speaking up and out, adjusting to change in their lives, or coping with a tragedy. Some face unforeseen challenges, and others hear and respond to new callings.

Besides the changes in the lives of individuals, there are changes and challenges in the life of a congregation as a whole. Every now and then there will be a disagreement, which may become a full-scale fight. Ministers come and go. Or things happen in the city or the world that demand a response from the church.

In all this a congregation is like a village. It is a community that exists through time. It both changes and stays the same. Logically it's impossible that something can change and stay the same, but in reality it happens. A river, to mix my metaphors, does that. It is both constantly changing and yet stays the same.

This village, like others, also has its own village elders, healers, characters, and even a village idiot or two! (Sometimes the minister fills all of these roles!)

I am sure you have heard the expression, "It takes a whole village to raise a child." It is an African proverb that means that the task of teaching skills, values, and a way of life to a child is too big for even two parents. We need others to learn from and live with. We need a larger story and framework of meaning than the family alone ordinarily provides. The church is that kind of village. The church is a community of people who are trying to live and teach a particular way of life, a way of life shaped by Christian beliefs and practices.

There's another, not as well-known, African proverb that makes a point similar to the one about the village. "A person is a person because of other persons." We might adapt that to the church to say, "A Christian is a Christian because of other Christians." Being a Christian is not easy. We need the help, encouragement, support, and example of others. Moreover, being a follower of Jesus has, from the beginning, been something that is done in community, with other people, not in isolation.

As a village or community that lives and teaches a way of life, the church may be an anomaly in today's world. There's a great word, "anomaly." It means "a deviation from the norm." Another way to put this would be to say that the church is a little odd. (I expect you've thought that yourself a time or two!) What's normal in our world today is constant change, lots of choices, the expectation of quick results, and the idea that we should be in control of our lives. Of course, there is some truth and value in these things, but probably less than we've been led to believe.

A good deal of what we're up to in the church goes against the grain of the world and always has. We are in the business of change, change in people's lives, but we recognize that this often takes time, possibly a long time. If you insist on quick results you may find the church frustrating. Also, we tend to value commitment as highly as, or more highly than, choice. And when it comes to being in control of our lives, the church is likely to remind us that we're not. Not in control, that is. The church does its work of changing human lives slowly. We tell stories, celebrate sacraments, and keep rituals. We talk and we work together. We sing and we worship. We are like a village, the village it takes to raise a child.

But there's something else that needs to be said. Some villages, communities, and churches are healthy and happy, while others are not. Why is that, do you think? What makes some churches and communities healthy and others not?

My observation is that healthy churches and communities are hospitable to strangers, while unhealthy and unhappy ones are suspicious of strangers. Also, in healthy churches and communities grudges and hurts are healed and released, while in unhealthy ones grudges and hurts are held onto and nursed. Healthy churches tend to welcome new life, while less healthy ones do not.

It may be for these reasons that most churches have a steeple or a spire or simply a cross on top. All of these are built-in reminders that we need to stay open, and that healthy villages and churches are not closed, but open. Open to new people and new ideas, without worshipping the new. Open, most of all, to the holy power from which life itself comes, and which is the source of the church's life.

I think of the steeple or the spire or the cross as a kind of lightning rod, only in this case the purpose is not to channel the power safely into the ground like a lightning rod does. The steeple, spire, or cross is more like a lightning catcher, ensuring that we get zapped or jolted on a regular basis. The spire or the steeple reminds us that what real power the church has does not come from within, but from without, from God.

Of course, lightning is strong stuff! It can give you quite a jolt. It can start a fire. And fire can destroy. But fire (often in the Bible fire is a symbol of God's presence) can also purify. The dross (the accumulated junk) is burned away, but the pure gold or silver stands revealed for all to see.

So the church, when it's true to itself, is a place of both comfort and challenge. There's village-like comfort. Here we know and are known by others. Here we are valued and loved. Here there's continuity, stability, and security. But it's not all comfort because this village has a lightning catcher on top. Here we will also be challenged, stretched, asked, and sometimes compelled to take risks, to change, and to grow.

Moreover, this village, when it's doing its job, will always be sending its people out into the world rather than keeping them safely at home. People from this village called church will have been touched, changed, and charged by being a part of this village where the lightning strikes. They will go out from it like explorers, prophets, teachers, and healers to touch others as they themselves have been touched by the power of God.

LOVE, DAD

10 · Worship

DEAR LAURA,

Do you remember when you completed the application for the Spectrum Program? You were asked to describe a special interest of yours. You picked reading. You *are* quite a reader. You are hardly ever without a book, and often seem to be reading three or four books at the same time.

What I found so interesting about what you said on the Spectrum application was the reason that reading is important to you. You said, "Reading gives me another world." That's a great insight, wonderfully expressed. And you're right. Reading can be like stepping through the wardrobe door into the land of Narnia. Suddenly, we're plunged into a different world.

For me, and I don't think I am alone in this experience, worship is something like that. We step into a sanctuary or chapel and it's a little like walking through the wardrobe door. There's music playing, different light and colors, strange words and stories. Not always, but often, I feel a presence. I am alert.

Now this may sound far-fetched to you. Maybe "going to church" hasn't ever felt like this—yet. (Or maybe it has.) But as life goes on, as you become involved in all sorts of things and have the usual worries, you may one day find that worship *is* like stepping through the door to a different world, a world where we see ourselves and others, and even life, a little differently. A world where we are caught up in a special and wonderful story.

There is a danger in this. It's also a danger in reading, in playing games, and in all sorts of activities. The danger is that we step through the doorway to a different world and it becomes a hiding place. A place to escape from life and all its problems. Some people say that's all church and religion are—an escape or a hiding place for people who can't face the real world. And sometimes when people say this they are right. Church does get misused that way.

I have told you that when I was a teenager I spent some time, maybe a lot of time, hiding. I was afraid, I guess, that people wouldn't or didn't like me, or that people would think what I said was dumb or not worthwhile. And sometimes I was afraid of exactly the opposite, not that people would not like me, but that they would like me too much. I felt that way about girls, who seemed to be interested in me many years before I was interested in them.

It's not always bad to hide. Sometimes we need to step back and figure things out. I always thought tree houses were neat for that reason. I built a tree house when I was your age. For me, it was a sanctuary. Worship has, at times, been like that, a place to step back and figure things out, to regain perspective. But church and worship never let me stay there. Over and over in different ways, church has been a place where I have been challenged. Challenged to emerge from my shell and make new friends. Challenged to try new things. Challenged to say what I think. Challenged to take a stand. And in fact, when I was a teenager and feeling like hiding, church was the place, more than anywhere else, that helped me come out of hiding, and to try my wings.

In your reading, you may have noticed that there is a pattern to many stories. The stage is set, the characters introduced. The plot is developed, and the characters interact and may change. Finally, there is some sort of conclusion to a story, an ending. The same is true for worship. There is a pattern to it. While different churches have different ways of worshipping, and from Sunday to Sunday, worship may very somewhat in the same church, overall and most of the time there is a pattern to it. It is a pattern with four parts.

The first part is praise or adoration. Our attention is shifted off ourselves, and onto God. Sometimes there is a rousing hymn, or the organ plays in such a way that it feels as if we are in the presence of something large and wonderful. Or we say words of praise, or pray a prayer of adoration.

The second movement is confession, confession of who God is and who we are in relation to God. Sometimes that happens in the words of a prayer. Sometimes in silence. Sometimes in a song. The third big movement in the pattern of worship is sharing the Word of God, in the Scripture reading, in the sermon, and in the sacrament of communion. (Every now and then in the Bible God says to someone that it's not enough just to hear the Word, you need to eat it, to swallow it and take it into yourself.)

And then the fourth and last movement: We are sent out. Sent forth into life and into the world to take our place there as cocreators with God, and coproclaimers of God's word of truth and love and mercy for the whole world. Those are the four basic movements. In different churches they do them different ways. Some kneel. Some stand. Some sing. Some chant. Some tear chunks of bread off a loaf, some eat thin, little, round wafers. Some preachers shout and sing when they preach. Some talk quietly. But the four movements are usually there. Praise, confession, sharing, sending.

Have you ever noticed how going into the sanctuary in our church could be thought of as something like going into a womb? How the sanctuary is rounded, and you enter it by going through a sort of hallway that could be thought of as a kind of birth canal? And at the entry point there is the baptismal font, full of water.

Going to worship is a little like going back to the womb, back to where we are dependent on something or someone else. We all need that at times in our lives, no matter how old or grown up we are. But we don't get to stay there. We get rebirthed, reborn, sent back into the world to stand on our own two feet and to be independent. That is the deep rhythm of the Christian life. Back and forth. In and out. Dependence and independence. Tending to our roots, spreading our wings. We need both.

The life of worship is like that. As you said of reading, "It gives me another world." So worship, with its four parts, gives us another world, another story. The great story of God's persistent and surprising grace. And then we go back into the ordinary world, but we are not quite the same. We have been changed, transformed, by that different world and different story.

I hope you will always be able to find a worshipping community that offers you this.

LOVE, DAD

11 · The Church Year

Dear Laura,

You remember, I am sure, the wreath of greens with four purple candles that takes its place on our table at home early each December—the Advent wreath. Do you remember also the three brightly colored kings, each astride a camel, which show up on our mantelpiece after Christmas? And perhaps you recall, too, the shimmering red, yellow, gold, and white streamers that appear in the sanctuary at church in the late spring? The first of these, which are hung right after Easter, are white and gold. As the weeks pass yellow, orange, and red appear until sometime in late May or early June it looks almost like tongues of flame are shimmering above our heads.

All of these are reminders of different times in the church year. The wreath with its purple candles is for Advent. The three kings are for Epiphany. The tongues of flame are for Pentecost.

You may also have noticed the way I've used the word "remember," or some form of it, several times already in this letter. That's one reason for the Church Year. It is, among other things, a memory device. A way of remembering and retelling the story of Jesus, and letting that story and its seasons shape our lives.

We all live with and by a number of different calendars. There's the calendar that ends a year on December 31 and starts a new one on January 1. Then there's the school calendar. For that one the year begins in September and ends sometime in June. There are fiscal (financial or budget) calendars that run from July to June. And if you are a baseball fan the year starts when the teams head for spring training in February and ends with the final out of the World Series sometime in October. There is also the agricultural calendar, with its seasons of planting and harvest.

All of these calendars provide a pattern and a rhythm to life. All of them remind those who live by them of important days and seasons. All of them shape the lives of the people who keep and observe them.

The church too has a calendar and a year of its own. Like all the other calendars, it reminds us of important days and seasons. Over time it can get into your heart and your bones and becomes a part of who you are.

Our Church Year, like so much about Christianity, had its origins in Judaism. The Jews too keep days and seasons as a way of remembering their story and of retelling their most important story, the Exodus story. The Church Year did not happen overnight, nor at the time of Jesus. Only as the decades and centuries passed did the Church develop it. By about the sixth century of the Common Era it had taken the shape and form we know today.

There are seven seasons to the Church Year. One way to think about the seasons of our year is with the symbol and metaphor of light.

The Church Year begins in late November or early December, four weeks before Christmas, with Advent. Advent, at least in the Northern Hemisphere, is the dark time of the year. One way to think about Advent is as a time of waiting for the light to come, or for the light to be born. During Advent we wait and prepare for Christ's coming.

A few days after the winter solstice, the shortest day of the year, is Christmas—the celebration of the birth of Christ or of the coming of the light. For Christians Christmas is not, however, only one day. It is twelve days. Twelve days to celebrate and feast after Advent's waiting and watching.

Christmas ends and the next season, Epiphany, begins on Epiphany Day, January 6. That's the day for telling the story of the three kings, or the magi, who came to visit the infant Jesus. Though they were not themselves Jewish, they came seeking the one who would be called, by some at least, "the King of the Jews." Moreover, the coming of these exotic foreigners signals something important. God's light is for the whole world, not just one people or nation. "Epiphany" means "revealing" or "manifestation." During the weeks of Epiphany that follow January 6 we tell the story of Jesus' baptism, of his early preaching and healing, and how light seems to blaze forth both from him and from all that he did.

But whenever light shines in a place that has been shadowed or dark, not everyone likes it. Rats run for their holes, and roaches for cover, when the lights come on. And people who have been doing things under the cover of darkness, so to speak, are exposed. That's a way to think about the next season of the Church Year, Lent.

"Lent" comes from a medieval English word which means "to lengthen," and during Lent the days are (again in the Northern Hemisphere) growing longer. It is almost as if light and dark are vying with one another. And so, during Lent, our focus shifts to the stories of the opposition to Jesus. When Jesus forgives and heals people, some people—usually the religious and political authorities—are disturbed. They are accustomed to having the power. But here was Jesus who also had power. He used it to do things that he said should be done by those in power, except they were misusing their power.

Lent culminates with Holy Week. During that week the Church remembers and retells the story of Jesus entering Jerusalem on Palm Sunday, teaching in the Temple, eating a last supper with his disciples, then being tried and put to death. The light has been put out.

Easter dawns, and with it come these astonishing words. "He is alive." The light has returned and will never be extinguished. "Jesus is risen." The powers of hatred and evil in the world are real, but not final. Maybe because this is such an astonishing message, Easter is not a day, but a season. We need time to digest it, to let it change us. Eastertide lasts seven weeks.

It is over these seven weeks that the color of the shimmering banners in our Sanctuary change from white and gold, the color of Easter, to yellow, orange and finally, red. Red is the color of Pentecost. "Pentecost" comes from a Greek word meaning "fifty," and is the fiftieth day after Easter.

According to Luke (see Acts 2) the disciples were all together on that day when they heard a sound like the rush of a mighty wind and saw what looked like tongues of flame resting about the heads of each of them. It is the Holy Spirit, sent from God and Jesus, to fire them up and fill them up for going out to do and say the same things Jesus himself had done and said. With Pentecost, the Church is born.

These six seasons—Advent, Christmas, Epiphany, Lent, Easter, Pentecost—take about six months, from early December to early June, each year. What about the rest of the year, the other six months?

That is called "Ordinary Time," and is our seventh season. The church goes forth, during Ordinary Time, to preach, teach, heal, and serve in Jesus' name. But with a difference. The difference is that having told the extraordinary story of Jesus for the first six months, we now see that in a way even ordinary times and ordinary places are no longer plain or ordinary. Every place and every day is, at least potentially, a place or a day where we can encounter God, and in which holy and wonderful things can happen.

In a way the Church Year is all about remembering—remembering our story, and remembering who we are. As a Native American writer, Leslie Marmon Silko, puts it, "The stories aren't just entertainment. They are all we have, you see, to fight off illness and death. You don't have anything if you don't have the stories." So the Church Year unfolds as the telling of a story, our story and God's story.

LOVE, DAD

12 · Prayer

Dear Todd,

I am eager to write to you about prayer for a couple of reasons. For one, prayer is perhaps the most important way for us to grow in our relationship with God. As Christians we may spend a lot of time learning about God, but that is not the same as having a relationship with God—much as you can learn a lot about a sports star by reading a couple of biographies, but that would not be the same as knowing him as a friend. It is important to worship God; if our worship is not centered in prayer, however, God can seem as distant as a relative you have heard a great deal about but have never actually met. Christians are called upon to serve God, but prayer is a way for us to know the God we serve, which can itself deepen our commitment to service.

I am also eager to write about prayer because, in my experience, prayer is often misunderstood. At least, I know that I held misconceptions about prayer for many years. Of course, I learned something about prayer by growing up in a church. Strangely enough, however, some of what I picked up about prayer in that setting actually kept me from experiencing prayer in all of its depth and power. In the church in which I grew up, prayer always seemed like a formal occasion. Usually it was one of the ministers who offered the prayer. It seemed as if prayer were a foreign language that not everyone knew how to speak. (For instance, God was always addressed as "thou." I never heard that word used anywhere else and I certainly never used it myself!) There also seemed to be a special technique to prayer that seemed beyond most people. After all, why else would they always ask the minister to offer the prayer? And most of the prayers I heard were eloquent, using the kind of beautiful speech that has to be thought out carefully ahead of time.

It really wasn't until I went to divinity school that I began to experience prayer in a different way. That didn't happen in a class (few of my most important spiritual lessons were learned in class), but when I met for prayer with a small circle of friends once a week. I think all of them were more experienced in prayer than I was, and seemed more comfortable with prayer as well. I remember feeling uneasy when we started out, not knowing quite what I was getting into. I'm not sure that I would even have joined the group, except I liked the guy who invited me.

The format of our meetings was very simple: we talked with one another about what was on our minds and then we talked to God. Sometimes what we shared was our concern about some situation in the world; other times it was something about what was going on in our own lives or the lives of people we cared about. What struck me was how little difference there was between our conversations with one another and our prayers to God. In both conversation and prayer we shared from our depths about what was most important to us. We spoke freely. Nothing was scripted. We didn't use a special language. There wasn't a "thee" or a "thou" in sight! This was something new for me and it was wonderfully freeing. For four years I met with that group. Some of my most treasured relationships were forged in that setting, including my relationship with God.

I later learned that Jesus' own teachings on prayer emphasize its simplicity. When Jesus' followers asked him to teach them to pray, we can almost imagine them taking out pencils and pads of paper to take notes on the extensive lecture they expected to hear from their teacher. What Jesus gave them, instead, was an example of prayer, a simple prayer that we call "The Lord's Prayer" (we call it that because Jesus taught it to us). In that prayer Jesus did not use the fancy and formal language of the temple, but the language of the people. Don't let those "thous" and "thys" fool you. Those translations into English date back to a time when those terms were as familiar as our words "you" and "your."

In translation, we begin the prayer, "Our Father . . ." This may sound like a formal form of address (at least, I can't remember the last time you addressed me as "Father!"), but the word Jesus actually used was much different. He began his prayer by saying *Abba*, a word that means something more like Daddy or Papa. It was a familiar form of address that one might hear from an infant because it resembles the early gurgling sounds that precede speech (babies often make noises that sound like, "abba . . . abba . . . abba"). In a sense, then, Jesus is saying that even infants who have not yet learned how to talk have sufficient vocabulary to approach God in prayer! And we are invited to have the kind of intimate relationship of an infant being held by his papa.

So prayer is not a formal address or a special technique. It is more like conversation with one who knows us well. But how does one begin such a conversation? Here are a few suggestions:

Begin where you are. Most conversations start out slowly, and sometimes even awkwardly. I once had a conversation with someone who, at the time, was beginning to take some tentative steps toward God in her life. She said that she was still not ready to pray. The prospect of approaching God in that intimate way still seemed too overwhelming. What she did feel able to do was this: at various moments during the day she would pause and say to God, "Hello," and then scurry back to whatever she was doing. It was nothing more than that, just a shy and simple word. I told her that I thought it was a good place to start. After all, many relationships do not start with a long conversation. As with so much in life, the most important thing is to start.

When you wonder what you should say in a prayer, don't begin by looking far and wide. Begin by looking at whatever is in your heart—whatever needs, whatever joys, whatever confessions, whatever concerns you may hold there. None of us can run out of such raw material for prayer, any more than we could run out of thoughts. Have you noticed that people who trust one another—good friends, for instance, or a husband and wife—never run out of things to say? They don't weigh words carefully because there is nothing to be held back. They just share with one another whatever is on their minds. Such is the kind of conversation that can develop between you and God, when you begin with what is in your heart and entrust God with it.

As I learned from that small group in divinity school, it can help to pray with people who have more experience in prayer than you do. Being in the presence of those who are comfortable with prayer can help put you at ease, much as it can help to listen in on a conversation before trying to jump into that conversation yourself.

You may notice that prayer is a conversation that falls into some familiar patterns. Being aware of these elements can help you express your thoughts in prayer. There is *praise,* in which we express gratitude for who God is, and *thanksgiving,* in which we thank God for what God has given us. (I once asked a group of kids what prayers they know by heart. One boy, trying to get a laugh, said, "Ruba dub dub, thanks for the grub. Yea, God!" I told him that it was a good example because it included thanksgiving *and* praise.) There is *petition,* in which we ask God for things and confession, in which we share with God all the ways we have messed up and ask for forgiveness. Finally, there is *intercession,* in which we pray for others. These five elements of prayer are not like a check-list you must fill out every time you pray. Nevertheless, an ongoing conversation with God that is rich and full will contain them all.

Sometimes our need is so great that we cannot put a complete sentence together. But God is not concerned with the words we use. In fact, some of the most powerful prayers are those that have no nouns, but rather consist only of urgent verbs such as help, listen, heal, and forgive. If we use the language of the heart, we may even abandon words entirely. The Apostle Paul said that sometimes our prayers are in the form of sighs, because what we experience is too deep for words. Some prayers may be like sitting in silence with a friend, a kind of conversation in which words are not necessary. Then too, in the silence, God can have a chance to speak to you. Perhaps God won't use words. At least, God has never addressed me using words. But I do know that some things have become so clear to me in a moment of prayer that it is as if God has spoken.

I have found that prayer, even more than other good conversations, is endlessly interesting and enriching. So I hope that, as the years unfold, you will share what is most important in your life with God in prayer, so that God's life might be shared more fully with you.

Love, D.

13 · Music

Dear Laura,

Every now and then, when I am leading a memorial service or a wedding, and we sing a hymn, I notice that a lot of people in the congregation are not singing. They stand mute as stones, face forward. That could be for any number of reasons. They may be emotionally overcome. Or maybe they are people who are unaccustomed to worship and to the music of the church. But sometimes I suspect it is something far worse: they have forgotten how to sing.

One of things I most love about the church, and for which I am grateful, is that it gives me the opportunity to sing, and to sing with other people. Of course, congregational singing is hardly the only kind of music in the church. There are organ preludes, string bass solos, and horn concertos. Choirs sing cantatas and soloists belt out spirituals. But congregational singing is the biggest part of it. And in North America today, where so much music is recorded or performed for audiences, the church may be the one place where people still sing together week after week and year and year in order to express their hopes and faith.

Most of what we sing in church are called "hymns." What makes a hymn a hymn? How does it differ from any other song? A great fifth-century teacher of the church, Augustine, defined a hymn as "a song of praise addressed to God." It is a definition that has stood the test of time, even if not all hymns are, strictly speaking, praise. Sometimes they are laments, the cries to God of people who know sorrow and suffering. Other times they are thanksgiving, or petition (asking God for aid for ourselves), or intercession (bringing the lives and needs of others before God). But all are songs "addressed to God." In singing hymns, whenever and wherever we do, we make an altar to God and lift up the world and our lives before the Holy One.

Another thing about hymns: most of them are prayers. In fact, Augustine also said, "Whoever sings, prays twice." Some churches have special books of prayers or prayer books that people follow during the worship service. But in our church and many others the hymnal is our "prayer book." It's powerful to think about a whole congregation praying together as they sing. If you want to pray, or to learn to pray, the hymnal may be one good place to start. Pick out a hymn that says what you want to say to God, and pray it. (In the Bible, the Book of Psalms is the Bible's collection of hymns, and they too are prayers.)

More than anything else besides the Bible and its stories, hymns form, shape, and express our faith. For example, take the twenty-five most frequently sung or favorite hymns in our church or any church. Study them to see what they say about God, about human beings, and about life. When you are done you will have a pretty good idea of the most important faith themes and beliefs of that particular church.

Hymns and music go very deep into people. That's one reason that using new hymns, or changing familiar ones, can be risky business. We become deeply attached to hymns. One year we used some new lyrics to some of the well-known and best-loved Christmas carols. Mistake. Some people just stopped singing and looked angry. Some sang the old words. Others looked as if their best friend had just died.

I've heard stories of people who have Alzheimer's disease or another brain illness that has taken away their memory and ability to know themselves or other people. They may not have spoken for months. Yet when their family has visited them and sung Christmas carols, they have joined in, and known every word. The words of the hymns were "written on their hearts."

A big question for the church today, and really always, is how much should what we sing or play in the church be influenced by what is popular in our society? As one person put it, "How much does Saturday night have to do with Sunday morning?" Would you be interested in hymns that sounded like some of your favorite groups or bands?

This is not a new question. Many of the tunes of our favorite Christmas carols were once popular drinking songs (songs sung in taverns) long ago. That is still happening, as new words are written to go with familiar folk and rock music today. It is a dilemma. Does the church pick up the music that is popular now so that when people come to church they feel the music is familiar? Or does the church teach and pass on a body of music and hymnody (the collection of hymns) that is its own? Over time the answer has been "both." But it's always a balancing act. If you use too much of what's current and popular, you risk losing your heritage. Or as someone said, "Those who marry the spirit of the present age are widows in the next!" On the other hand, if you don't use any of it you risk cutting yourself off from the world and culture around you.

Another interesting question is about hymnals themselves. Of the two thousand years of the church (three thousand if you count our parent faith, Judaism), hymnals as we know them have been around for maybe four hundred years. Do you have to have hymnals? On one hand, they are powerful and much loved collections and, as I've said, "the prayer book of the church."

Having hymnals generally enables congregations to sing a much wider variety of music than would otherwise be the case.

But some congregations have never used or relied on hymnals. They learn their hymns by heart. There's something wonderful about that. Still other churches, in a more recent change, have stopped using hymnals and instead they project the words to hymns on large video screens, figuring that many people are more comfortable looking at a screen than a book.

In our church we are accustomed to using hymnals and I expect we will probably continue to do so. But I can see value in other ways. For one thing, if you aren't holding a hymnal, you are free to clap and freer to move your body with the music.

One night when I was at a church in Nicaragua the lights suddenly went out all over town. It was dark, very—very dark. Some people hurried to find candles. But most of the congregation, which had just begun going through a line to pick up their dinners, began to sing, loudly and joyfully. It was amazing. We kept on singing in the dark until candles had been lit to go on with dinner together, and after a while the lights blinked back on.

Ever since then I've thought that was a wonderful image for the church: people who sing with joy even in the darkness. Sometimes life can be very dark. Challenging things happen. Terrible things happen. There are times when we feel very uncertain about the future. The hymns of the church have sustained people in the dark times of their own lives and in the darkest times of history. Music has an incredible power to enable us to go on and to renew us.

What are your favorite hymns? Which ones do you know or would you like to know "by heart"? I hope that singing will always be a part of your life.

Love, Dad

14 · Baptism

DEAR TODD,

I'm sure that you don't remember anything about the day of your baptism. You were, after all, only a few months old at the time. I remember it very well, however, and not just because it was the only time I have ever seen you in a dress! (Actually, it was a long baptismal gown that Gramme had made; all of her grandchildren wore it for their baptisms, so at least you were in good company.)

I remember the day because it was a singularly joyous occasion, a day full of promise and full of promises. Your mother and I promised to raise you in the Christian faith and in the nurture of the church. The congregation promised to share with you the cost and joy of discipleship. The most important promises offered in your baptism, however, were not our promises, or the congregation's promises, but God's promises. Through your baptism, God has promised you many things.

For one, God has given you a name. We baptized you using your name. This is the way the Christian Church signifies that God knows your name. Of course, we can know someone in a vague or passing way without knowing his or her name. But our God is not an impersonal force or a distant being. God relates to each one individually, even intimately. To say that in baptism God gives you a name is to say that in baptism God joins in that kind of personal relationship with you. Even before you know your own name, God knows it. Even before you could possibly know what it means to love God, God loves you.

Also, in baptism you are given another name, the name of Jesus Christ (in fact, some people speak of baptism as being "christened"). When I placed the water on your head, I said, "In the name of the Father, and of the Son, and of the Holy Spirit, one God and Mother of us all." You are given Christ's name in baptism in that you are his. He has a claim on your life. Christ's name is now a part of your name and you will carry it about with you always, even in the very word, "Christian." To be baptized in Christ's name means to participate in his life. Some Christians are immersed in water when they are baptized, as Jesus was. As the water folds over them, they are surrounded and sealed by water, as if in a watery tomb, or in the womb, only to rise again to breath the air of new life, a resurrected life, the life of Christ. It may seem strange to offer new life to one whose old life is not very old yet, but it is an unfolding promise that is available to you when you need it, as all of us do at some time or another.

Part of what it means to be baptized, to be offered a new life even before we fully need it, is the promise of God's forgiveness. Through baptism we are reminded that, just as we use water to wash ourselves, through the waters of baptism God promises to wash us clean even when we have made a great mess of things. I realize that when you were baptized you were still too young to have had much opportunity to make a great mess of things, but it is also true that we are each born with a leaning toward sin, almost as if it is another one of those things that is already part of us from the beginning. We all wrestle with the unfolding of that tendency as we move through life. In baptism, however, we recognize and signify that God's forgiveness is as much a part of our lives as is our tendency toward sin, and indeed overcomes it. That is why you are only baptized once: God's promise of forgiveness need only be made once because it is a promise that will not be broken.

Another promise God offers in baptism is a new family. It is the family of faith. When you were baptized the members of the congregation promised (there's that word again!) to receive, nurture, and befriend you in the Christian church. It is something of an adoption ceremony. In a sense, on the day of your baptism we agreed to put you up for adoption by a church that promised to love and nurture you, come what may. They welcomed you as a family welcomes a new baby, with all the joys and added responsibilities that that new relationship entails. And the family you joined that day is a large one. In your baptism you were initiated into Christ's family, Christ's Church universal, which includes Christians of every belief and practice.

Beyond all of this, in baptism God gave you one further promise, the continuing presence of the Holy Spirit. The gospel accounts say that at Jesus' baptism the Spirit descended upon him like a dove. At your baptism God skipped the dove, but the Spirit was there all the same! This gift of the Holy Spirit is very important because it is through the Holy Spirit that God can be an active, creative presence in your own life. God is not only distant and awesome, but through the Holy Spirit God is as near as your own breath (which is another image used in the Bible to describe the Spirit).

As I say, it was a day filled with promise and promises!

I want you to understand how significant it is that your mother and I would bring you to the church to be baptized. Like most parents, we feel very protective of you. A day or two after you were born we brought you home in a big plastic bucket they gave us at the hospital. It was battleship gray and seemed as sturdy as a battleship also. It was filled with a nest of brightly colored blankets and pillows so that you could stay warm and your head wouldn't flop around. I'm sure that, if we had any, we also would have used some of those Styrofoam peanuts that are used for packing fragile and precious items. We buckled that car seat in just right and made sure that it was secure, as carefully as if we were sending you to the moon in a space capsule. And then we drove home more slowly than you have ever seen me drive since.

For the most part, that loving, protective concern doesn't change all that much as you get older. You've seen this, of course (or, you might say, "put up with it"). Before we drop you off somewhere, we want to know something about who will be in charge. After all, in some way we are entrusting you to their care, if only for a time. We won't entrust you to just anyone. So it is significant that, on the day of your baptism, in the most profound way, we entrusted you to the God we know in Jesus Christ. You and Alanna are the most precious things in the world to us. We love you so much, and so want good things for you. We also want you to be safe and to be cared for. And on the day of your baptism we said something like this: "We entrust this little one to Jesus. In this dangerous and treacherous world it is to the care of Jesus that we entrust this son of ours."

As you know, when you wake up in the morning with "bed-head" (what other people call "a bad hair day"), often I will take some water in my hand to smooth down a cowlick and say as I do, "I baptize you in the name of the Father, and of the Son, and of the Holy Spirit." Usually I say it in a light-hearted manner, as if it were only another of our shared jokes. But, to me, it is also a wonderful moment in the day as I remember the day when I slathered your hair with the waters of baptism. Indeed, I can think of no better way to start the day than with a reminder of the promises of baptism!

LOVE, D.

15 · Communion

Dear Laura,

When I was two or three years older than you are now, the youth group at the church in which I grew up had its own communion service. One evening we pushed twenty chairs or so into a circle in the chancel of the church's sanctuary. We were led by our assistant minister, but otherwise it was just us kids.

As the bread was passed around the circle, one young woman, Barbara was her name, shook her head to say "No" when the bread came to her. She wasn't going to take communion. She sat in a deep and thoughtful silence. I learned later that Barbara felt she was not deserving of communion that night. It was strange, because she was one of our best and brightest. Either she felt she had done some particular thing that disqualified her, or she was just generally out-of-joint, spiritually speaking.

I don't know which it was, but I remember being impressed. I guess that's obvious since I have remembered it for all these years. Barbara's refusal of communion seemed, somehow, the expression of a deeper or better faith than that of the rest of us who shared in the sacrament without much thinking about it.

Over the years, I've come to a different view. I've decided that Barbara was, in her own conscientious way, missing the point of communion. We don't qualify for this meal any more than we qualify for our place at the family table. It is gift. Grace. It is given to us, by Jesus, not because we are such good Christians, or good people, but precisely because we're not.

Many years after that communion service with our youth group I read something written by a woman named Nancy Mairs who put into words what I'd been thinking. She wrote that she came for communion not because she was "a good Christian, but because she was a bad Christian." She may have been exaggerating to make her point. What she meant was that she came for communion because she needed forgiveness and she needed grace. She needed God. If she were perfect, or had it all together on her own, why bother?

Communion began this way. The very first time the sacrament of communion occurred was at Jesus' very Last Supper with his twelve disciples. He knew something that they didn't, or at least if they had any idea of it, they weren't yet able to face it head on. What Jesus knew is that one of them, Judas Iscariot, had already made a deal with the religious and political leaders in Jerusalem to betray Jesus. Moreover, Jesus knew that when the net began to tighten around him, the other eleven would either run away or pretend they had never known him.

In other words, the congregation at the very first communion was a lot like every congregation since then. It was made up of people who had done wonderful and courageous things. Many of them had given up a lot to follow Jesus. But still, they were capable of absolutely awful things too. Things like betraying their friend and teacher, and lying by saying they had never been with him. They, like us, were a mixed bag—capable of great good and great evil, of beauty and ugliness.

Still, as they finished their meal together that evening, the special Passover meal that all Jews were eating that night, Jesus took a loaf of bread, blessed it, broke it, and gave it to them saying, "This is my body, broken for you." When they had finished the bread, he took a cup, poured wine into it, and said, "This is my blood, shed for you."

It must have been confusing, even frightening, to his disciples. What did he mean by these strange words? Why was he doing this?

But ever since then, from those first disciples at the Last Supper until now, the church has believed this about communion: knowing our failures and fears, Jesus still gives himself to us and for us. He doesn't wait until we get good enough or perfect or until we understand everything he meant. He just gives himself to us.

It is another way of saying, this time without words, that the way God loves us is unconditional. God's love for us, and for all, comes first. And it comes last. God's is the first word, and the last word.

In many churches communion is a part of the worship service every

Sunday. That's probably the way it was in the first couple of centuries of the church's existence. Believers came together to hear the Scriptures interpreted in a sermon, and to receive the broken bread and the cup of wine in the sacrament. They listened to Jesus, then they ate with him.

Over the centuries, however, the church divided over, among other things, the meaning of communion. It's a long story, and I won't try to tell it here, but one way to simplify it a little is to say that some churches—mostly the Protestants—put primary emphasis on the interpretation of Scripture, or the sermon part. Others—mostly Catholics—put the main emphasis on the communion part. Neither side had it right, at least not completely. Both had it about half right, which is usually the way it is in family fights. Each side has a part of the truth and mistakes that part for the whole truth.

One of the reasons that both sermon and sacrament are important and belong together is that we human beings are complex creatures who do not get it just one way. Most of us need to have things taught and explained to us. While that's not everything that a sermon is, it is certainly part of it. But words and explanations alone are never enough. Sometimes you can't explain the meaning of something only in words. You have to show someone what you mean. You can tell someone you love them, but showing it speaks too. And that, in a way, is what communion is—God showing us how and how much God loves us.

Something that is hopeful today is that the two sides in this family fight seem to be coming together and appreciating each other's truth. It is a slow process, but again, simplifying a bit, the Catholic part of the family is paying more attention to the sermon part of the service. And the Protestants (we are in that crowd) are paying more attention to the sacraments and to communion. That seems right to me. We need words—to hear God's story. We also need to be shown—to taste God's love and to share it with others, as we would share a meal.

It is hard to say exactly how communion works, that is, how it communicates God's love and presence to us, or how it changes us. But I know one thing for sure: as people come forward and as I offer them the bread and say, "The body of Christ, broken for you and for us all," something happens. People are touched. They are fed in the deepest and most surprising ways. We somehow know that we are connected, to God, to one another, often in ways that we had forgotten. Somehow the broken bread and the poured cup help us to become more whole and holy.

LOVE, DAD

16 · Confirmation

DEAR LAURA,

Most Protestant churches have two sacraments, baptism and communion, and a handful of rites and rituals. Some of these rites and rituals are weddings, memorial or funeral services, reconciliation or healing services, and ordination. Probably the ritual of the church that has been more worried over, tinkered with, and wondered about than any other is confirmation. People have wondered, among other things, what is the right age for confirmation? Who should teach it? What, exactly, should be taught or learned?

Some churches have very clear answers to all these questions about confirmation. It is a two-year program, taught by the pastor, which meets every Saturday morning and covers a clear and definite list of subject matter. Other churches have no answers at all, and some have given up on confirmation altogether. It has proven too difficult to carve out a regular time or to arrive at something everyone can agree upon as the right age or the right materials for study.

When this much confusion exists it is sometimes helpful to go back to the roots of a thing, to its origins, and to basic questions. When you do that, and go back to the origins of the word "confirmation," it is interesting to discover its meaning. It means "to strengthen." Confirmation is, or perhaps should be, the church's effort to strengthen young people during the wild and wonderful ride of adolescence, and for the journey toward becoming adult people. It is the church's best effort to strengthen young people by helping them understand and know something about the people and practices of the Christian faith.

I have noticed that often the church has it backwards. We seem to think of confirmation as a time when teenagers tell us adults and the church what we want to hear. We think of it as a time for teens to confirm or affirm the church. There's an element of that, but mostly it gets the emphasis in the wrong place. The emphasis needs to fall on our best efforts as a congregation to strengthen young people, a part of which is affirming your capacity to make decisions.

Usually confirmation does take place in the early teen years, say ages twelve to fifteen. Some argue that this is the wrong time. "Kids are too unstable at this age," say some, as if teens were a volatile chemical (which maybe isn't too far from the truth!). Or "This is a time for rebelling and questioning everything," say others, "not for making commitments." Surely, a part of the problem and confusion is that in our American society, adolescence has been stretched out to age eighteen, twenty-one, twenty-six, or even thirty-five. The time of adulthood, the process for becoming an adult, and even what is meant by "adult" are all up for grabs in contemporary America.

But for centuries and centuries in all sorts of cultures and communities, this age, roughly the age of puberty, has been a time when cultures have shared their stories, their secrets, and their mysteries with their young. It is part of the process of becoming an adult. Bodies are changing. Physically, you are no longer children, but not yet quite adults. Cultures and religions the world over have chosen this time to recognize, honor, and bless these changes and to acknowledge them with rites of passage.

How do we go about this strengthening work, this confirming work, in the church? It does vary a lot from church to church and denomination to denomination. A great deal of what I see us doing at our church has to do with stories and relationships.

We adults share the stories that give life meaning and that speak to the deepest human questions. We share the church's story and God's story. For the most part, the Bible is God's story, the story of what God has done. Knowing what God has done helps us to understand what God is doing. We learn the patterns of God's activity by studying and learning this story.

The Bible is not an easy book, nor a straightforward one. But that is part of what I love and treasure about it. It is a frothy stew, full of rich, thick, textured stories, most of which cannot be whittled down to just one meaning. Part of confirmation is exploring more deeply, and learning, these stories. Think of yourself as a Hopi, a Navajo, or a child on the island of Crete, learning the stories of your people. The Bible is not only that, but it's a place to begin.

In addition to the biblical story and stories, we try to see that you know more about the story of our particular family of faith or denomination, the United Church of Christ, and of our congregation, Plymouth Church in Seattle. More than we present-minded Americans know, history lives on in each of us. We are shaped by our past whether we know or not. Usually it's better to know it than not.

We also go about this strengthening work by opening a door for important relationships. As you know, each one of you who is in confirmation at our church has an adult mentor. Among other things, adolescence is a time when a certain distance opens up between parents and children. But teens still need reliable and trustworthy adults in their lives, so we hope to invite that possibility by having mentors. It is their job to get to know you, to help you get to know them, and to learn from their example and experience what it means to be a Christian in today's world. We also hope that a sense of community and bonds will develop between all of you in the confirmation class, and that you will become in some way special to one another.

In addition to the stories and relationships the church makes available to you through confirmation, it also offers you a specific rite of passage, a time in which you stand up in front of God and the congregation to be seen and blessed and acknowledged for the adult you are becoming. We touch your forehead with water from the baptismal font to remind you of your baptism and the ways that God's grace has been active in your life even before you were aware of it. We lay hands upon you, which is a gesture that has to do with conferring and transferring power, and we pray for each for of you by name. We pray that God will guide, sustain, and direct your life and bring you, in the end, to life everlasting in the glorious presence of God and all God's angels. Then we have a party at which you are the guests of honor.

One of the reasons some churches have given up on confirmation is that young people and their families have often confused confirmation with graduation. After confirmation they are never seen again. I suppose that's a danger in having a focused program or a big moment. But in reality confirmation is not a graduation or an ending. It is more an entry and initiation, and a beginning.

It is a beginning in a couple of ways. Now, you are invited to take your place in the congregation and church as a person who has gifts to share and a contribution to make. You can become a full, voting member of the congregation. I have seen young members of the church speak a decisive word at a congregational meeting, lead the church in prayer, come up with a great mission project, and set aside a percentage of the money they make for the church.

It is also a beginning, more than an ending, of a faith journey that will take your whole life to complete. To be confirmed is to say that you intend to pursue your faith journey and spiritual growth within this congregation, this tradition, and this faith. That may not remain true for your whole life. Who knows, you may become a Buddhist or a Jew. You may find your spiritual home in a Twelve Step Group, or do all your worshipping on long hikes in the mountains. But for now, being confirmed means that you join others in seeking to grow and practice your faith in this congregation and in the church.

But there's an even deeper way in which it is a beginning. While confirmation doesn't mean this for everyone, it is for some an act of deep trust, a giving of yourself to God, as you understand and have come to know God. It is a saying "Yes" to something beyond yourself.

There is, in us humans, both a need and a capacity for self-giving, for offering ourselves, to that which is greater than ourselves. Even as, at adolescence, we are often pretty focused on ourselves, we may have a powerful intuition that the very best way to find yourself is by giving yourself.

Jesus said something like that, "Whoever would seek to save their own life will lose it, while whoever loses their life for my sake and the sake of the gospel shall find it." It's a paradox, something that isn't logically true, but is true in all the ways that matter. Or at least that's been my experience.

Love, Dad

Letters about the Bible

17 · Favorite Bible Stories

Dear Laura,

"Favorite Bible stories?" Golly, that's a hard one. There are so many.

There are verses I hold close like, "For I am convinced that neither death, nor life, nor angels, nor rulers, nor things present, nor things to come, nor powers, nor height, nor depth, nor anything else in all creation, will be able to separate us from the love of God in Christ Jesus our Lord." (Rom. 8:38–39). Or "We do not live to ourselves, and we do not die to ourselves. If we live, we live to the Lord, and if we die, we die to the Lord; so then, whether we live or whether we die, we are the Lord's." (Rom. 14:7–8) There are the Psalms, like Psalm 23, Psalm 27, Psalm 121, and Psalm 139—some of my favorites.

But stories? There are so many. The stories of the old geezers Abraham and Sarah, and their trickster grandson, Jacob. There's the novella that is Joseph's story in the book of Genesis. Moses at the burning bush, and the wild tales of the prophets, Elijah and Elisha. Naboth's vineyard and Namaan the Syrian general are two great ones. I love the stories of Ruth, of Jonah, and of Esther.

And then there's the New Testament. The stories of Jesus, who is kind and encouraging to people that others shun or despise, like Zacchaeus, the runty little tax collector, or the Samaritan woman, or the woman caught committing adultery. I love the story of Jesus on the Emmaus Road, walking alongside two of his discouraged disciples, who do not even recognize him. Then, of course, the parables. The parable of the waiting bridesmaids, of the vineyard workers who are all paid the same, of the wedding feast, and of the sower who tosses seed, with abandon, everywhere.

I could go on, but you are probably getting blurry-eyed already, so I'll settle on two stories of Jesus that have meant much to me.

The first one is told by Matthew, in the fourteenth chapter of his Gospel, though similar stories are found in Mark and John also. The disciples were out on the sea, rowing for all they were worth, and getting absolutely nowhere. A strong head wind meant they were rowing in place. They saw someone walking toward them on the water. Quite naturally, they were terrified and thought what they saw was some sort of ghost. But it wasn't. It was Jesus.

When Peter realized who it was he said, "Lord, if it is you, bid me come to you on the water." And Jesus said, "Come." So Peter threw his big feet over the side of the boat, planted them firmly on the water, and began to walk toward Jesus. Peter was doing it—walking on water—until he realized what he was doing and, noticing the wind, took his eyes off Jesus and began to sink.

I think of it as something like learning to ride a bike. The first time you are really going on your own, you realize what you're doing and then you fall over.

The story of Peter walking on water is a wild one, one that makes a lot of people uncomfortable because they just don't get miracle stories. But the idea that Jesus calls us to step out of the boat—which is safe, even if it isn't going any place at all—makes sense to me. Most of us like to find a safe place, which is okay. But mostly God doesn't let us stay there long. One way or another, we are challenged to step out of the boat and try something we've never tried before, or to do something that is "impossible."

I've always loved Peter because he seems game for these adventures. It's true that, before long, Peter is up to his neck in the dark water and crying out for help. But at least he tries. And for a moment he even does it. He walks on water. He did it just so long as he kept his eyes and his heart fixed on Jesus. When he got distracted, when he paid attention to the howling wind, it was all over. Glub, glub, glub.

I've stepped out of the boat a number of times—when your mother and I got married, when I became a father, when I went to seminary, when I became a minister, when I've led congregations in new ventures, and in a hundred smaller, daily ways. Often enough I've ended up in the drink, calling out for help. And usually it is because I've taken my eyes off the source of love and hope, and paid attention to my fears instead. Every now and then, however, I have planted my feet on water and walked. When I haven't, or when I get scared, I've been pulled out, put back in the boat, and before long invited to try again.

Another story that means the world to me comes from Mark's Gospel, chapter 6, although parallel accounts can be found in Matthew, Luke, and John. It is one of the Bible's best-loved stories for lots of people—Jesus feeding the five thousand.

But that title alone doesn't tell nearly the whole story. Jesus had been teaching that day to a huge crowd. They were off in some isolated, desert-type place. As the day wore on and night was coming, the disciples began to get uneasy. They were worried that they would have a big problem on their hands when the crowd got hungry and there was nothing to feed them. So they said to Jesus that he might want to send the crowd on its way before it got even later so that they could find a Burger King or something and get dinner.

Jesus, as he often does, surprised and maybe even toyed with the twelve. "Why don't *you* give them something to eat?" he said. "Us?" they answered, mouths hanging open in disbelief. "Why, it would take ten, maybe twenty thousand dollars to feed all these people!" "Well," said Jesus, "why don't you take a look and see what you've got."

So they did, and they came up with five loaves and two fish.

Should you become a teacher, or a minister, or a pianist, or a parent, the day will come when you look at the hungry crowd sitting before you and realize that what you've got to give them isn't much. You realize you don't have nearly enough wisdom or faith or talent or love for the need that is there, for the hunger that surrounds you and is inside you.

At which point Jesus says, "Let me have what you've got." So, you push your little loaves and dried out fish into a pile and you present it to him. When we give what we have to Jesus, and entrust it to him, he manages to do things we had never thought possible. Our little turns out to be enough, more than enough, when Jesus takes it, blesses it, breaks it, and gives it to the hungry.

There have been a fair number of Sundays when what I had for a sermon seemed pretty measly fare. Not nearly enough for all the hungry people. I understand those disciples. Hungry people can scare you. If you can't feed them, who knows, they might just eat you. But it is surprising how often, on those Sundays when it didn't seem like what I had was nearly enough, I gave it to Jesus and people came away fed.

One of the things you get to learn as a parent, too, is that you don't have enough of whatever it is you need to raise a child. Nobody is smart enough, good enough, or patient enough for the job. In fact, being a father or a mother is a great way to discover your need for the help of other people, and for God's help.

Both of these stories—Peter walking on water, and the feeding of the five thousand—are called miracle stories, and they are. But when all is said and done, the miracle is not just about Jesus. The miracle is about you, and who you are and what you will do when you trust the power in the universe that is always on the side of those who are brave enough to trust it.

LOVE, DAD

18 · The Really Hard Parts of the Bible

DEAR TODD,

People who are familiar with the Bible usually have their favorite passages (Tony has written a letter to Laura in which he shares some of his). These are the passages that comfort or challenge, inspire or enlighten. Usually these are the passages people have in mind when they put the Bible close at hand on their bedside table. Nevertheless, anyone who has read much of the Bible also confronts the really hard parts, the parts that—for one reason or another, in one way or another—frustrate, baffle, or even offend. When we confront such passages we may not want the Bible on the bedside table, or perhaps even in the house. When I read passages like that I sometimes remember the famous book review in which the critic said, "This book is not to be tossed lightly aside . . . it is to be hurled with great force!"

It is important to remember, particularly when we confront the hard parts, that the Bible is not a single book. It is more like a library of books that were written by many different authors over a period of about a thousand years. There are books of history, prophecy, song lyrics, laws, love poems, sermons, legends, and letters. In some ways it is as difficult to summarize the Bible as it would be to summarize any library. Given such a complex variety of historical circumstances, authors, points of view, and literary forms, I suppose it would seem strange if there were *not* some hard parts. And there is such variety in the Bible that it makes sense that it is hard in a variety of ways.

Some parts of the Bible are simply *hard to understand*. For those who have not studied the Bible, much of what they encounter in this ancient and complex book could be described in that way. Most often, reading the Bible with a helpful guide is enough to make much of the Bible understandable. But study is not always enough. I have spent many years studying the Bible, but I still confront some passages, such as in the letters of Paul, that are so dense and convoluted that I have to read them many times. Even then I sometimes feel like such intense reading will make me go cross-eyed before it will help me understand a particularly difficult passage.

Then there are the passages that are *hard to relate to*. For instance, the book of Leviticus, in our Old Testament, was addressed primarily to the priests of the ancient temple in Jerusalem. In its original form, it is like a handbook that instructed the priests on everything from how to prepare an offering to how they were to wash their hands. Actually, further study reveals that much of this book is both important and interesting, but I have to admit that for years Leviticus seemed about as engaging and relevant to my life as reading the owner's manual of a tractor.

Other passages in the Bible depict things that are *hard to believe*. I will write you a separate letter about miracles, so let me just say here that I believe that God has the power to perform miracles. Indeed, the resurrection of Jesus itself is a miracle and I not only believe in it, I base my entire life on its reality. But some of the wonders recorded in the Bible are still hard for me to believe. For instance, one passage relates how the prophet Elisha was able to make the iron head of an ax float on the surface of the Jordan River (2 Kings 6:6). It's not that I don't believe that God could do such a thing through a prophet. Any God who can raise someone from the dead could make truckloads of ax heads float (or sing and dance for that matter) before breakfast, if God ever chose to do so. It's just that the story makes the act seem so frivolous, like a magic trick that doesn't accomplish much beyond impressing one's friends. I have a hard time believing in miracles that don't mean very much.

I also have a hard time believing that God would harden the heart of Pharaoh against the plight of the Jews held in slavery, as in the fourth chapter of Exodus, and then clobber Pharaoh with a series of plagues because he has a hard heart, as the sixth chapter reports. Here again, it's not that God doesn't have the power to do such things, but a God who would act in this way is very different from the God I encounter elsewhere, including elsewhere in the Bible.

Near the end of his life Thomas Jefferson spent a great deal of time editing his own version of the Bible. He took out all of the passages that he found difficult to believe or that offended his sensibilities. When Jefferson was finished, his "Bible" was only forty-six pages long (apparently Jefferson's sensibilities were easily offended!). By contrast, when I encounter such difficult-to-believe passages in the Bible, I have learned not to dismiss them entirely. After all, I am sure that God has done many things that I find hard to believe; God is not restrained by the borders of my imagination. But I don't pretend to believe things I don't believe, either. Instead, I try to keep such passages in the kind of place where I will be sure to pick them up again. I don't discard them, as Jefferson did. I treat them much like the pieces of paper on my desk that I am not sure what to do with—I neither file them away nor throw them away. That means that I look at them more frequently than I would papers that I had put in the file cabinet or the trash bin. That is, I try to stay open to new insight and understanding. In the meantime, I ask myself what is at stake in believing or not believing in something like Elisha's ability to make an ax head float. If I can't believe such a thing, is my faith in God shaken or my reliance on Jesus Christ lessened? Usually the answer is, "No, not in the least." That doesn't make such passages any easier to believe, but it can make it easier to live with my disbelief.

Finally, there are those passages in the Bible that are *hard to accept*. Usually such passages offer teachings that, for one reason or another, we cannot follow or would rather not even try to follow. For example, the book of Leviticus says that homosexuality is wrong and even advocates that homosexual people should be stoned to death (Lev. 20:13). I cannot accept that. It is passages like that that remind me of Mark Twain's famous observation that it's not the passages of scripture he doesn't understand that give him difficulty, it's the passages he *does* understand. I believe that this is an instance when, living in a different circumstance several thousand years later, we can see some things differently than did the authors of scripture.

It is harder for me to know what to do with other teachings. For instance, Jesus taught that married people should not divorce. His teachings on the subject were more strict and uncompromising than the standards he inherited. And we're not talking about some obscure verse from a book of the Bible hardly anyone reads. All four gospels record Jesus' teachings about divorce. Even Paul, who never met Jesus, quotes his teachings about divorce because he had heard what Jesus had to say on the subject. And this is Jesus they are quoting, the Man himself!

Nevertheless, when I am working with a couple whose marriage has become marred by some form of abuse or so riddled with conflict that the marriage seems like a death-match in which the parties can neither leave nor come out alive, it can be difficult to accept such a teaching, no matter the source. Sometimes I end up supporting a couple's decision to divorce. Even in such instances, however, I do not take out Mr. Jefferson's scissors to cut out the passages I find difficult to accept. I keep them close at hand because I recognize that my own perspectives are limited and I still have a lot to learn. I pray for fuller understanding and new insight. After all, we often learn the most from other people when we don't readily agree with them. Often that is true in our relationship with the Bible as well.

Although I do try to keep the really hard parts of the Bible close at hand, that doesn't mean that I dwell on them. In fact, I think the philosopher Søren Kierkegaard was right when he said that it seems strange that people complain that there is so much in the Bible they cannot understand or accept, when there is enough they can both understand and accept to keep them busy for a lifetime.

My hope is that, over time, you will develop the kind of relationship with the Bible that, even if you are occasionally tempted to hurl it across the room, you will keep it very close. If you do, I am confident that your life will be changed and enriched by the encounter. You will also find that the Bible is much like a dear lifelong friend: you may have your points of occasional conflict, but over time you will find that this companion is worthy of your deepest trust.

Love, D.

19 · The Apostle Paul

DEAR LAURA,

Of the twenty-seven books of the New Testament, fourteen were written by, or are attributed to, Paul. Two-thirds of another, the Book of Acts, is mostly about Paul. In terms of sheer pages, Paul wrote more of the New Testament than any other single author. The books of the New Testament that were written first were written by Paul.

You can't really come to grips with Christianity without coming to grips with Paul.

Who was Paul? Let's start by saying who he was not. Paul was not one of the twelve disciples called and chosen by Jesus himself. And, so far as we know, Paul did not ever actually witness Jesus during his ministry, during the time that Jesus taught, preached, or healed people in first-century Israel. So, it is pretty amazing that Paul became such a prominent figure in the early church. How did it happen?

Like many of the early followers of Jesus, Paul was Jewish. He came from the town of Tarsus. He had trained to be a rabbi, and he was a member of a Jewish group known as the Pharisees. Like all the Pharisees he was devoted to his religion and took it very, very seriously.

When we first meet Paul, in the early chapters of the Book of Acts, he is not a follower of Christ or part of the church. In fact, Paul is hostile to Christ, to his message, and to those who followed him. Paul was among the religious leaders who actively persecuted early Christians, beat them up, and put them in jail for their dangerous beliefs and activities.

One day Paul was on his way to the town of Damascus where he planned to round up the followers of Jesus and put them in jail. But on the road to Damascus, a strange thing happened. Paul had a vision. The light was so bright that he fell to the ground and was temporarily blinded. Out of the light a voice, the voice of Jesus, spoke to Paul and asked him why he was so filled with anger. The voice said that God had something very important for Paul to do. God intended for Paul, a man who had been filled with hate for Jesus and the followers of Jesus, to be filled with love and to be entrusted with the task of telling the non-Jewish world about Christ. Moreover, Paul would start the first congregations, churches, in the world outside of Palestine and Israel.

It took Paul a time to come to believe this, and it wasn't exactly easy for the early Christians to swallow either. After all, Paul had been enemy number one. But God can do that. God can turn enemies into friends. God can change hearts and lives.

Paul was changed, transformed. Where he had been Mr. Know-It-All, he became reliant upon others and upon God to lead him and teach him. Where he had been filled with hostility and anger, he became filled with faith, hope, and love. Where he had been trying to stamp out this new movement, the Church, he became one of its greatest leaders and thinkers.

It's quite a story, one from which many people have drawn inspiration ever since. But not everyone is a fan of Paul. I remember talking with a friend of your brother Nick's, a gal who came to stay with us a couple of years ago during the holidays.

She asked what I was going to preach about that Sunday. I said, "One of the letters of Paul." She then said, "I don't know the Bible all that well, but some of the passages I like most and some of the ones I really don't like at all, both of them come from Paul."

In my experience, she is not unusual. A lot of people seem to have pretty mixed feelings about Paul. Why is that?

My hunch is that at least part of it is that Paul is so embarrassingly human, his weaknesses as well as his strengths so evident for all to see.

Where Jesus manages to walk through a hostile crowd unscathed, Paul is forever getting pounded, beaten up, and run out of town.

Where Jesus is never self-justifying or defensive, Paul seems so often in his letters to be defending himself against his critics (who could be numerous), and in the process may not always seem all that appealing.

Where Jesus delivers his parables like a Zen master, Paul gives us labored and often convoluted arguments. His sentences seem at times to go on forever, and even if he hasn't managed to lose his train of thought, he does often manage to lose us.

Where you can make an argument that Jesus maybe did not intend to found a church at all, Paul travels all over the Mediterranean starting congregations that are as conflicted, confused, and glorious as the man himself.

Where Jesus manages to pretty much avoid talking about sex, Paul is a good bit like my own parents were (and maybe like yours too), fumbling around trying to figure out what to say and managing to contradict himself on more than one occasion.

Despite all this, I am a fan of Paul. You sometimes have to work hard to clear away the dirt and debris, to get at the jewels of faith and wisdom Paul has to offer, but they are definitely there. And when you do work at it, the lesson Paul teaches that is to some his most offensive idea is also his best. It is this. We're not in charge. We are not God. Only God is God. God is in charge, not us.

Though Paul did not tell the following story, it is enough like what he has to say that he could have.

There were two battleships on maneuvers at sea. The weather was bad and so, as night fell, the captain of one remained on the bridge to keep watch through the patchy fog. Shortly after dark, the lookout on the wing of the bridge reported, "Light bearing on the starboard bow."

"Is it steady or is it moving astern?" called out the captain.

"Steady, captain" said the lookout, which meant that this boat was on a dangerous collision course with the captain's ship. The captain called out to the signal man,

"Signal that ship: We are on a collision course; advise you change course twenty degrees." A signal came back, "Advisable for you to change course twenty degrees." The captain said, "Send: I'm a captain; change course twenty degrees."

"I am a second class seaman," came the reply, "You had better change course twenty degrees." By that time the captain was furious. He spat out, "Send: I'm a battleship. Change course twenty degrees!"

Back came the flashing light. "I'm a lighthouse!"

"Change course twenty degrees," muttered the captain.

Paul's own experience had been like that of the captain of the battleship. Thinking that he was in charge, that he knew it all, he discovered that he wasn't and that he didn't. Then he spent the rest of his life speaking to others saying, "There is a lighthouse. It is Christ. Advise you change course. Now."

Paul made four different trips around the eastern end of the Mediterranean, in what we know now as Turkey and Greece. He started congregations in many cities and towns. Most of the books of the New Testament that Paul wrote are actually letters to these different churches that he founded.

In his letters he sounds like a mother or father, which in a way he was. He pours out his love. He gets upset about dumb things they have done that have ended up hurting themselves and others. He answers their questions about problems they are having. He encourages them. He explains his own faith, and helps them understand the faith.

Maybe the reason Paul elicits such mixed reactions is that he so often sounds like a parent. Many people react to him like most of us reacted to our own parents when we were teenagers. That is, we try to pretend we don't know them because they clearly don't know anything. But later in life we discover our parents weren't so dumb after all. In fact, they were pretty smart. I expect that for many Paul too seems smarter as we get a little older.

LOVE, DAD

20 · Miracles

DEAR TODD,

Occasionally I am asked if I believe in miracles. Often the person asking such a question has just read something in the Bible that he or she finds hard to believe: God parts the waters of the Red Sea so that the people of Israel can escape slavery in Egypt; a woman is healed by merely touching the hem of Jesus' cloak; Jesus feeds thousands of people gathered on a hillside with a couple of fish and a few loaves of bread. Often people want to know: Did such things really happen or are they just made-up stories? And if they really did happen, why don't we ever see miracles like that today? Has God gone out of the miracle business?

When I am asked if I believe in miracles usually I get the impression that people want a simple "yes" or "no" answer. So, in case you are wondering, yes, I do believe in miracles. But for you to understand my response I will have to say a bit more.

In one sense, I don't think it is particularly difficult to believe in miracles. The word "miracle" literally means, "a sign that points to God." A miracle is anything that reveals God to us. So we are surrounded by miracles every day. When you were born, a beautiful, screaming little bundle of life, I knew that I was in the presence of a miracle. The way the human body can heal from injury or disease is a miracle. That we can experience the love of another person even when we are not being at all lovable is a miracle.

Some people are so open to the presence of God in the world that they are able to see miracles—signs that point to God—all around them. But most of us are not that attentive and receptive. After all, if we were completely tuned into God's presence in the world at every moment, it would be quite overwhelming. It would be like being able to hear the grass grow—so overpowering that eventually we would have to tune it out.

So most people miss miracles. They see them but they don't see them. Sometimes our ability to close out miracles can be so extreme that it is almost comic. I remember one example from a television show called *Candid Camera* that was popular when I was your age. The program used a hidden camera to catch people doing funny or embarrassing things. In this instance, they rigged an artificial flower at a lunch counter in such a way that it could rear up out of its vase and "drink" from the glass of a customer sitting at the counter. As I recall, some people responded by staring at the flower or by complaining to the waitress. But what I remember most clearly were those people who didn't respond at all. They saw the flower drink out of their glass but it didn't seemed to impress them as anything out of the ordinary. They saw it but didn't really see it. One man was slurping soup and reading the newspaper when the flower started to "drink" from his glass of milk. He responded by moving his glass out of range of the flower and going back to his reading!

The *Candid Camera* flower was not a miracle, of course. It was just for laughs. But it does remind me of the ways in which we can see and yet not really see. In the case of miracles, often we see what has happened but do not see God in it.

So it's not surprising that the spectacular miracles that Jesus performed often were lost on those who saw them. Even Jesus' closest followers seemed to miss a lot along the way. They were present when Jesus multiplied the loaves and fish so that the crowds could be fed. They had picked up the baskets of scraps that were left over after everyone had their fill. And yet the disciples seemed not to catch on. Later, when Jesus asked them to recall what happened, they simply reported the facts: there were five loaves for five thousand people and they took up twelve baskets of scraps. In other words, they could do the math, but they didn't pick up on what else was going on. Jesus had given them a stunning glimpse of God's power and all they could see or remember was a picnic in the sun. God's miracles don't always impress us. Perhaps it's not that God doesn't do miracles anymore but that we simply don't see the miracles God performs. It may be more our problem than God's!

Even if you and I were convinced that we would not miss the miracle of loaves and fish multiplied, I am quite sure that we miss miracles every day. There are miracles, signs that point to God, all around us every day. It's as if God said, "I will give them a sign. I will make plants to cover the earth in a thousand shades of green. It will be a feast of green. And for those who live in the desert, I will make it up to them in the spring when the parched land will explode with the color of wildflowers. And I will create animals and birds and fish of every description. And I will make ostriches, just to show that I have a sense of humor. And I will give them food to eat, and people to love, and I will show them a still more excellent way, so that they might have life and have it abundantly." And yet, living in the midst of such miracles, people often say, "If only we had a sign. Then I could believe that God is at work in the world."

The trouble with that kind of approach is that it reveals a misunderstanding of the relationship between faith and miracles. People often say something like, "If I see a miracle, then I will have faith." But the biblical story turns that approach on its head. The Bible makes clear that often it is only through faith that we can see a miracle in the first place. The old saying, "seeing is believing," becomes, "believing is seeing." After all, the naked eye is not enough to see something so magnificent as God's presence. Only the eye of faith is perceptive enough to see God at work.

Even the central miracle of our faith, Jesus' resurrection, was not seen by everyone. Not unlike the folks at the luncheon counter captured by *Candid Camera*, some had hearts receptive enough to see the miracle, while others dismissed it so immediately and so completely that it was as if they hadn't seen it at all.

When you were a young child, you believed in many things you did not see. For you, like most children, the world was an enchanted place. In the stories we read to you and the games you made up, wonderful things were possible: animals could talk, magic potions conferred special powers, and you could fly through the air to dunk a basketball over a seven-foot defender. As you grew older you left many of these understandings behind, shed like clothes that no longer fit you. Now that you are on the verge of adulthood you may be particularly eager to leave behind everything that might be associated with childhood. That means that this is a time when it may be most difficult to believe in miracles. After all, to believe in miracles may seem something like believing the childhood fantasies that you are eager to leave behind so that you might approach the world in what seems like a more adult way. If childhood is a time when you believed everything you were told, adulthood can seem like a time when you can only believe what you can see.

That process is understandable, of course. The problem is that some people assume that the I'll-believe-it-when-I-see-it approach to life, so often associated with adulthood, is the last stage of development. But something else is required of us to become mature Christians: we must circle back and reclaim some of the openness and receptivity of the child. (Or perhaps instead of saying we "must," I should say we "get to," because that is a wonderful and exciting way to approach life!)

I would not want you to believe everything you are told, as a child does, or believe only those things you can see, as many adults do. Rather, I hope you will have the kind of open and receptive faith that will allow you to see something wondrous that many people simply miss—God at work in the world, in the story that is told in the Bible, and in your own life, miracles all around.

LOVE, D.

Letters about Vocation

21 · Vocation

DEAR TODD,

When I went to seminary to study to be a pastor, people often asked me about my "call" to ministry. In that context, the word "call" reflects the understanding that one doesn't become a parish minister simply because one wants to. It is more than a mere career choice. Instead, God calls certain people to do that work. That doesn't mean that God speaks to them, at least not in words, because a call can take many forms. So when the people asked me about my call to ministry, they were asking how the sense of being called took shape in my life. They wanted to know how I came to understand that in some sense God was asking me to be a parish minister.

I do believe that God does call people for particular tasks. Let me quickly add, however, that some people make the mistake of assuming that this only applies to pastors and others who work in the church. God calls people to various tasks because there are many needs in the world. The need for leadership in the church is only one. There are many others. In fact, everyone is called to serve in one way or another. God has an important task in mind for each one of us. It is from this understanding that we get the word "vocation," which comes from the Latin word for call. In our time, however, often this understanding is lost.

Someone once shared with me a particularly powerful memory of something that happened when he was attending summer church camp as a child. At the closing campfire, the pastor who served as chaplain of the camp suggested that perhaps during the course of their week together some of the campers have heard God's call to service. Those who had were invited to come forward and say a word to the pastor. One boy approached the pastor and whispered something in his ear. The pastor then announced that "Michael" (or whatever his name was) had heard the call to become a parish minister. The pastor shook the boy's hand vigorously and said, "Congratulations, Michael!" A girl came forward next. She said something to the pastor, then the pastor reported to the gathering, "Susie has heard the call to be a medical missionary. Congratulations, Susie!" Then, when the pastor asked if anyone else had heard God's call, another boy came forward. He too whispered in the pastor's ear. The pastor responded by patting the boy on the shoulder. Then the boy sat down without another word being said. The person telling me this story was that boy, now a middle-aged man. There was still some hurt in his voice when he asked me, "Can you guess what I whispered in the pastor's ear? I told him that I felt called to teach mathematics."

Even as a boy, he understood something that the pastor did not: God doesn't only call people for service to the church. The world also needs people who understand math and dedicated teachers who view teaching as a high "calling" (there's that word again), so God calls people to those important tasks as well. Every Christian has a vocation, a calling, an invitation to use one's gifts in a variety of ways and through a variety of roles. People are in need of care and healing, so God calls some people to be nurses and doctors. The world is a dangerous place, so God calls other people to be lifeguards and firefighters. We were meant to live joyfully, so God calls pitchers like Pedro Martinez and musicians like Dizzy Gillespie.

I realize that many people don't approach life and work this way. They think of their job as something they have chosen to do for their own reasons. Their job is just a job. In fact, for many today the word "vocation" has come to mean simply, "job," and not, "calling." When we forget the religious dimension of the word vocation, however, we can lose the sense that our work is valued in God's sight, valued enough that God might ask someone to undertake it.

Something else important can be lost when we use the term vocation as just another word for job. We can forget that God often calls us to important tasks that are not jobs. A tollbooth collector may have difficulty in viewing her job as a vocation, as something she was called by God to do, but she may have a keen sense of God's call when she responds to the invitation to tutor young children in the inner city. Parents who stay home to raise children may not have a job outside the home, but they can have a powerful sense of vocation, of calling, about what they do. This also means that someone who is still in school, as you are, can have a vocation. God has something in mind for you, too. God calls each of us.

There can be a similar confusion about a related word, the word "minister." Just as some people seem to think that God only calls people for church work, they also use the term "minister" only in reference to someone who works in a local church. But, just as everyone has a vocation, so too everyone has a ministry. A vocation, a calling, is an invitation to use one's gifts in a variety of ways and through a variety of roles. Ministry is what happens when a person responds to that call through action. Vocation is God's call to us, ministry is our response to God. There is another word for those who accept the call to serve a local church by preaching, teaching, and extending care: pastor. A pastor is just one kind of minister, however. There are as many ways to be a minister as there are ways to serve God and other people.

Where our response to God's calling intersects with the needs of the world — that is where our ministry takes place. So there is no end to the variety of tasks that can be approached as ministry. Being a camp counselor can be a ministry. Making music can be a ministry. Being a good friend can be a ministry. In this sense, ministry looks a lot like people doing just what they would otherwise do, but there is this important difference: they understand what they do as God's work undertaken in response to God's call.

I find that an exciting way to approach life. Instead of pursuing just what we choose to do, we can try to discover what God has in mind for us, which often is much more interesting and fulfilling than what we would choose. Instead of approaching what we do as just another task, we are invited to see ourselves as God's special agents in the world, God's ministers.

I know that sometimes you are asked if you want to be a minister "when you grow up." I also know that, when I was your age, I was already tired of responding to that question. In light of what I have written here, let me suggest a way to handle the question the next time someone asks you. You can say, "Thank you for asking. But, you see, I'm already a minister." That response will either give you an opportunity to educate your questioner, or, if you choose not to say any more, it may leave your questioner so perplexed that that person wouldn't think of asking it again. I would encourage you to explain your response, but I also realize that it might be more fun not to!

I have left out of this letter anything about how you might figure out what God's particular call is to you. That's an important question that deserves its own letter, which I will write at another time. For now, let me say that I know that God has some special plans for you, some special tasks for you to take up. That is, I look forward to seeing what kind of vocation God has in mind for you!

Love, D.

22 · Why I Became a Minister

Why did I become a minister? Well, I had to do something! You've heard the phrase, "Necessity is the mother of invention"? Well, maybe necessity is sometimes, if not the mother, then the aunt or uncle, of vocation.

I was twenty-six years old when I went off to seminary (the kind of school where people prepare to be ministers). I had graduated from college four years earlier. Your Mom and I had spent a year living and traveling in Europe. I had gone to graduate school for two years, at the end of which I had a Master's degree in history, but no clear career goals. Then we lived in Hawaii for a year where I was a part-time teacher at a community college. During that year in Hawaii your brother, Joseph, was conceived. Your Mom was pregnant, I was soon to be a father, and I felt that I'd better get on with it. Whatever "it" was, it needed to include a way to support a family.

Since high school, I had thought, off and on, about becoming a minister. As a teenager I had gotten quite involved in our church youth group. I had been encouraged to do that by our minister, John W. He was an important person in my life. He saw potential in me and encouraged it. I saw in him a man who was bright and also kind. It was combination I admired, and I wanted to be like him.

As time went on I got to know other ministers to whom I also felt somehow drawn. Like John they combined intelligence and compassion. When

I was in college, and later graduate school, my own thirst for knowledge and joy in the life of the mind blossomed—so much so that I thought I might become a college professor. But something in me wanted more than the life of a scholar and teacher. I wanted to be involved in people's lives and in making connections between great ideas and ongoing life and events. I wanted to be involved not just in studying life, but in changing it. I saw this in the lives of the ministers I knew. They stood, or so it seemed to me, with one foot in the world of ideas and another in the world of human lives and communities, with their struggles and their challenges.

Still, neither the first reason—that I had to do something—nor the second—role models that I found attractive—were really sufficient reason to become a minister. You have to have faith! That I hesitated as long as I did before going to seminary and that when I went I did so with my fingers crossed, so to speak, was because I was unsure about my faith and beliefs, or even if I quite had any.

I did have a sense of the something holy, of what one writer I had read called, "the mysterium tremendum." I experienced this sense of the holy, of the sacred, in different ways and places—in nature's beauty and grandeur, in the vibrancy of cities, in art and drama and movies, in great events and movements of life and history, and in worship. But I was not able to really express what I experienced. Nor did I have any very clear beliefs about God, or Jesus, or things like that.

So when I went to seminary it was as if I were going to chefs school because I loved the taste and sight of food, but I didn't really know my way around a kitchen much at all. (Your mother would say that I still don't!) What I mean is that I didn't really know much about the Bible, nor did I have much understanding of basic Christian beliefs or what they meant, if anything, to me.

At the time, I had a lot of doubts because of this. Did I have any business going to seminary, I wondered? How could I possibly consider becoming a minister? Looking back, however, I am not sure it was such a bad thing to have these questions. I had a feel for the feast, even if I hadn't learned how to handle the utensils or know the recipes. Since then I've met many people who knew the recipes and tools well enough, but seemed to have little enthusiasm for the feast. For me, the three years of seminary began a lifelong process of learning the language, texts, history, and practices of Christianity.

I suppose that if I had bumped up against things that I really couldn't handle or accept, that would have been a problem. To be sure, there were lots of things I had questions about, but nothing that proved impossible. In fact, I found Christian faith to be a rich banquet. The stories of the Bible proved surprising and powerful. Theology and other subjects were challenging and engaging. I began to understand the meaning and language of worship. Even the history of the church was fascinating to me. Moreover, working in churches—which I began to do in my first year of seminary—felt right. Through it all, my vague sense of something holy, something sacred, began to find focus and greater meaning. Don't misunderstand me. I am not suggesting this is the way to go about it. Not at all. It just happened to be my way.

So, I had to do something, and several attractive role models were ministers, and then, I experienced a gradual conversion of my general religious feeling into a more focused faith. What else figured in my becoming a minister?

Somewhere along the way I had learned that the word "religion," in its origins, is related to the word "ligament." Ligaments are those parts of the body that hold muscle and bone together and allow them to work together. "Religion," like "ligament," had to do with connections, with holding things together, and with seeing the sometimes hidden connections between different things and people. As a student of history I had discovered my own love and knack for this—making connections, seeing patterns and relationships.

Moreover, as a young man I had the feeling that our society and people in it were becoming "disconnected." It was the time of the Vietnam War, and then of a sorry political scandal, Watergate. These, along with several other things that had happened, left a lot of people distrustful. Everything seemed to push people to think about "me," not about "us." But what most moved me was the big picture, the connections. I felt that life without something larger than the individual person, some larger sense of purpose and meaning, was a life of poverty. Not material poverty but spiritual poverty.

Speaking of poverty, I was aware that ministers didn't make a lot of money and that you shouldn't go into it expecting to become wealthy. But as early as high school I had somehow come to the conclusion that if your goal was to make money most anyone could do that. There was no big trick, I decided, to making money. The trick was to do something with your life that was interesting, challenging, and might make some difference. Has the ministry been that for me? Yes, it has.

Another thing that appealed to me about being a minister was that ministers don't do just one thing, or even two or three things. They do lots of different things, even in the course of one day. As a minister, you are a preacher and a teacher, but also a counselor and a community organizer.

You're a leader and a bit of an actor. You're a writer and a fund-raiser, a planner and a poet. You are present in people's lives at times of great joy and deep sorrow. You work with eight-year-olds and eighty-year-olds, and every age between. You're a part of public life and of private lives. There's a pattern to it, but no one day is the same as another. This appealed to me.

Of course, you might wonder what holds it all together? It is this, I think. Churches are vessels, or containers, for human change, for helping people face their (and our) problems, and for helping people grow in honesty, in love, and in trust in God. All the many different things a minister and a church do have to further this purpose.

While I was thinking about what to write in this letter, I tried an exercise called "Random Words." It's a little crazy, but it's designed to get you to think about things from a new or different angle. Here's how it works. Say you have a topic or a problem you're pondering. You open up a dictionary wherever you happen to open it. Then without looking you plop your finger down on a word. You read the word and its definition and ask yourself what in the world that has to do with your topic.

So I tried it. I fingered the word "placoid," which means "plate-like, as in the hard, tooth-like scales of a shark, skate, or ray." "Why I Became a Minister" + "placoid" = What?

Here's what. My own family, for its particular set of reasons, didn't encourage a lot of tenderness or openness. My skin was pretty taut by the time I left home. In college and then graduate school I discovered and sharpened my intellectual capacities. My taut skin became, however, more placoid and plate-like in the process, and with intellectually sharpened teeth. I found I could keep others at a safe distance, and even hurt them, with my wit and intelligence.

When the road forked and one way led to college teaching and scholarship, and the other to ministry, I chose the latter at least in part as a way of shedding my placoid skin. I recognized that I could go through life with a hard skin, or, like a snake, I could shed that old skin and leave it behind. For me, becoming a minister was something like shedding an old skin and learning to live less by fear and more by trust.

Love, Dad

23 · What It's Like to Be a Pastor

Dear Todd,

Every year Alanna's school has a "Career Day." It is a time for students to learn about a variety of careers and perhaps to determine what career they would like to pursue. In advance of that day the school invites parents to spend a portion of the day at the school talking with students about their own professions. Each year, when the form requesting parent volunteers arrives, I fill it out, listing my vocation as "pastor," and each year they don't take me up on my offer. It doesn't bother me, really. I have come to see it as a reminder that being a pastor is, well, different. It's not the sort of job that anyone would be expected to pick out on a "Career Day."

As you know from observing me, pastors work long hours and we don't have the luxury of being able to leave our work at the office. There are times when all of the competing demands on a pastor's time can seem relentless. And, for this, most pastors aren't paid as well as we would be if we pursued other careers. Pastors used to enjoy a particularly respected and honored place in society, but even that seems to be changing.

So, if Alanna's school ever asked me to talk with students on a "Career Day," I would probably say something like, "Don't become a pastor unless you feel you have to." After all, by most measures the pastoral ministry may not be a very good career choice. But here's the difference: if you feel in

90

some way compelled to enter the pastoral ministry (that is, if you have concluded that God has called you to this work), it can be a wonderful life's work. Indeed, I wouldn't trade it for anything.

Fred Buechner, a friend you may remember meeting when you were younger, once wrote, "The place God calls you to is the place where the world's great hunger and your deep gladness meet." His words capture well my experience of being a pastor. Among the many needs in a person's life, none is greater than our need for God. Most of us long for the presence of God with a deep, aching hunger, a hunger as sure as the hunger for food.

Saint Augustine, who lived in the fourth century, observed that each of us is born with an empty place in our hearts that is in the shape of God, and that means that nothing and no one else can entirely or ultimately fill it. This empty space is not a square hole, or anything so simple as that, but a complex, hungering, God-shaped space where only God fits and which only God can fill. We can try to fill that space with other things—human relationships, careers, or other pursuits—but sooner or later they will leave us unsatisfied.

So what I find most gratifying about being a pastor are all the ways I am given an opportunity to help people encounter God and deepen their relationship with God. Of course, I don't make anything like that happen. My role is much more limited than that. In some ways I think of my role as more like a midwife, someone who is trained to assist in the birthing process. A midwife performs her role in a whole range of ways: sometimes by coaching the parents and other times by providing some direct assistance, and often, when little needs to be done, simply by standing by in wonder and awe.

In the case of pastors, we assist people in "giving birth" to a new or deepened relationship with God. We are not the center of the action, or even key players in the drama. Like midwives, our role is limited but can be quite important nonetheless. We perform our role in a variety of ways—for instance, by teaching, leading worship, and visiting the sick. We tell the Christian story, coach and encourage, listen and pray. What unites all of these roles and activities is that each provides an opportunity to encounter God. Even church committee meetings—to pick an unlikely example—can be the setting for such an encounter when we ask, "Where is God in this? What might God say to us here?"

It is a joy simply to be present at a birth. It is something even more—a real privilege—to play some part, however small or incidental, in that birth. Actually, in my work as a pastor, often I am not aware that anything so momentous is taking place. But then someone will report, fresh from a kind of birth, that a particular worship service helped her experience Jesus Christ as a living presence, as if for the first time. Or a young person returning from a church service project will tell the congregation what it was like to encounter Jesus Christ disguised as one of the poor. Or someone will tell me that my prayers at his hospital bedside provided ongoing comfort because, when I left, I seemed to leave God with him.

In each of these instances I am very aware that I did not make anything happen. Sometimes, like a midwife, my role is limited to holding a hand and offering a few words of encouragement. Nevertheless, something I did not provide, something clearly beyond me, that "something" called the presence of God, was at work. On those occasions I realize that I can no more take credit for the encounter than a wick could take credit for a flame or a cello could accept praise for a sonata.

So, much of the time, I feel like an invited guest to special places where wondrous things happen. I am not invited because I am a special person, or because I have a particular set of skills, or because I have greater faith than anyone else does. I don't think of myself as a holy man. Nevertheless, I am invited to those special places in people's lives because I have accepted God's call to do this holy work. As I have written to you elsewhere, God does not only call pastors. There are other kinds of important work to do, even other kinds of work that can be called holy. Nevertheless, almost every day I am grateful that I was called to be a pastor. Although it can be challenging work, it also is a great blessing to be called to a place where "the world's great hunger" and my "deep gladness" meet.

A great pastor, Harry Emerson Fosdick (who was your grandfather's teacher and mentor), said on the occasion of his retirement, "If I had a thousand lives to live in this century, I would go into the parish ministry with every one of them." That's quite a statement! If I had a thousand lives to live in this century, I might use one or two to do something else, like become a jazz pianist or an NBA point guard. But, with just one life to live on this earth, I am grateful that God had the role of pastor in mind for me.

Love, D.

24 · God's Call to You

DEAR TODD,

In a previous letter I shared my conviction that everyone has a vocation, a calling. In this letter I want to say something about how you might go about figuring out what your vocation is.

For some people, this is not difficult. I know people, and perhaps you do too, who have always known what God would have them do with their lives. They cannot remember a time when they were not sure about the direction of their lives. They might talk about it in different ways (saying things like, "I always wanted to be a doctor," or, "I feel like I was born to be a parent"), but what they communicate is that their sense of vocation was always a part of their experience, almost as if it were in their genes.

Other people I know tell of experiences in which they discovered, in a single dramatic moment, what their vocation is. You know the story about our friend, Jerry G., who was a lawyer, and not unhappy with the practice of law. But then, one day, he went to pick up one of his daughters at a birthday party. The children were playing outside, so he sat down at a table with another father at a table where the children had been playing with modeling clay. As they chatted, Jerry picked up a piece of the clay and began to mold it into a figure. As he tells the story, in that moment he knew that this is what he wanted and, in some way, needed to do with his life. He continued to practice law part-time for a while but, as soon as he could, he quit his law practice entirely so that he could devote himself to his sculpture. His vocation, his calling, as a sculptor has been his full-time job for twenty years now.

I imagine that it must be wonderful to have that kind of certainty about one's vocation, to know one's calling from before the beginning, or to know it in an instant. That has not been my experience, however, and that is not the experience of most people I know. Most people have to do a bit of holy detective work to figure out what their true vocation is. A famous Christian philosopher, named Søren Kierkegaard, said that each of us is born with sealed orders and it is our lifelong task to figure out what those orders are, even as they remain sealed. But how does one go about doing that?

Well, first of all, I believe that God calls us to the place where our particular gifts meet the world's great needs. God does not call us to meet needs for which we have no particular gifts. For instance, there is certainly a need for scientists to discover the cure for cancer. But, of course, that does not mean that everyone is called to that kind of work, because not everyone has the gifts required for such an endeavor. By contrast, people may have a particular gift for something, but not have a sense of vocation about what they do, if they do not see that what they are doing meets a great need. For example, your mom has an extraordinary gift for writing complex technology contracts, yet she often yearns to do something else because she is not convinced that it makes any real difference in the world. She knows that she has a gift, but she is not sure that what she does in her work meets a great need in the world.

So one of the ways to begin to find out what is in your sealed orders is to learn more about the needs of the world and your own gifts. For most people, the needs of the world are more obvious than their gifts. And, for most of us, it takes time to discover our own particular gifts. One of the reasons you take classes in so many different subjects at this stage in your education is to learn more about your gifts. By building mechanical devices, some people learn that they are gifted at creatively addressing technical challenges, as a teacher once said of you. By writing essays, some people discover that they have a special ability of expression.

As our education continues and our experience broadens, our understanding of our own gifts can become more clear and focused. For instance, a friend of mine knew from an early age that she had a special gift for writing. Throughout her youth and early adult life other people, seeing her great gifts, encouraged her. Nevertheless, even though she wrote short stories and poems for quite a number of years, few were ever published. Today, however, her writing is widely read and praised. One might even call her famous. The difference? Today she writes essays, instead of short stories and poems. She found her particular gift. At first she knew that she had a gift for writing and only later learned that she had a gift for a particular kind of writing.

For most of us, clarity about our vocation unfolds over time. We may not know what we are to do with the rest of our lives, but we can have a sense of what we should do next. As a wise person once put it, God does not so much give us a search light as a pen light. That is one reason why the "what do you want to be when you grow up?" kinds of questions are so unhelpful (and usually annoying as well!). Such questions do not let God's will unfold over time.

So it is important not to hold too tightly to your own ideas about what God's particular call to you may be. And it is just as important not to adopt any other person's idea of what your vocation might be. For instance, I know of people who ended up as teachers because they always said they would be teachers, or as lawyers simply because other people were sure that they would make good lawyers. For most people, neither holding tightly to one's own perception nor adopting someone else's is the best way to discern to one's true vocation.

Nevertheless, it is important to add that the observations of other people can be helpful, particularly because we are not always the best judges of our own gifts. Other people can see things about us that we cannot see our- selves. For instance, I think some of your special gifts are a discerning ear for music, a keen wit, loyalty, and a sense of justice. You also have a particular ability for analytical thinking, friendship, building things, and buying pres- ents. Does anything in my list surprise you? Perhaps I have seen something in you that you have not yet seen.

I gather that your friends have told you that you are a good listener and have an ability to help others with their problems. Someone even gave you the nick-name, "The Psychologist." That doesn't necessarily mean that you should become a psychologist, of course, but does that perception others have of you reveal anything about your particular gifts that you might not have known otherwise? Sometimes God speaks through the perceptions of other people. Listening to them, and being open to hearing God's voice through them, may help you discern what is in your sealed orders.

As I said in my previous letter, one's vocation is not necessarily the same thing as one's job. Some people find their vocation in the workplace, while others sense God's call in other areas of their lives. Whatever the setting, however, vocation is found at the intersection of our gifts and the world's needs. In my own experience, and in the experience of others I know, one knows when one has found that intersection when there is a sense of rightness, fit, and — perhaps most telling of all — joy.

There is joy in using God's gifts to help address the needs of God's world. There is no joy quite like it, in fact. So I look forward to seeing your sense of vocation unfold in your own life, both so that the world might benefit from your many gifts, and so that you might experience the joy of responding to God's special call to you.

Love, D.

Letters about Relationships

25 · Family

Dear Todd,

The word "family" is used in a lot of different ways these days. Churches, clubs, and other organizations sometimes describe themselves as families. I once saw a recruiting poster in a fast food restaurant, which read, "Why not join the [insert company's name here] family? We offer excellent benefits!" When we changed heating oil companies at home, I got a letter from the company president, which said, "Welcome to our family of satisfied customers!" (I thought that was a bit much. I just wanted to buy oil from the guy, not have him join us for Christmas dinner!)

When organizations describe themselves as families, I think they are trying to say that they affirm strong ties and care about individuals. They want to communicate that they are *like* families. The only trouble with that comparison is that *nothing* is like a family. Not really.

There is an old expression: "You can choose your friends, but not your family." That is how a family is different from other associations, too. You can choose to give your business to an oil company, or choose to join a club, but you cannot choose your family. The members of your family are given to you. That is another way of saying that you're stuck with them. That is how families are different, and it makes all the difference. That is both the challenge and the blessing of being part of a family.

At their best, families encourage both the ties that are held in common and the individual lives of their members. Common ties are important. I think of those times when we have watched family slides at family gatherings in Pennsylvania. We see the old pictures and laugh at the old stories, many of which have become very familiar by now. Have you noticed that the stories don't wear out, as jokes do, but seem to become all the more treasured as they are repeated? On those occasions I have seen you listen and laugh at those stories, even though most of them took place before you were born, because in some sense they are your stories too. Shared stories are part of what it means to be a family.

Also, most families hold something like common values. When you have asked your mother or me to explain why we do certain things, or why we want you to do certain things, sometimes we have replied, "Well, that's what we do in this family. That's the kind of family we are," as if that were explanation enough. I realize that that is the kind of parental response that drives most kids crazy (including me, when I was a kid!), but it is a familiar way of pointing to shared values and convictions that make a particular family different from other families.

Nevertheless, at their best, families do not expect everyone in the family to be alike, to enjoy the same things, to have the same gifts, or to want the same things for their lives. I have noticed that when families have found ways to accept such differences, they can even come to view that variety as something like a gift.

At their best, families are safe havens. A family is a place where you don't have to explain everything. It is where you can be yourself, for better or for worse, and usually it is both. When we are in the world, most of us wear something like a mask much of the time. The mask is not intended to deceive, but perhaps to show only the aspects of ourselves that we want to show, usually our competent selves, our polite selves, or whatever "self" helps us get along in the world. Most family members know each other too well and have seen one another in too many different circumstances to bother with masks anymore. That is, at their best, families are where we can be more completely ourselves. That can be wonderfully freeing and, when we feel accepted within the family, it also helps us interact with others outside the family with more freedom.

At their best, families are where we can experience something close to unconditional love. We are stuck with our families and, at their best, family members love the ones they are stuck with. We don't love family members because they are compatible, or because we like them, or because we enjoy their company, but because . . . well, because they are family. There is a givenness to the love for family. It is beyond reasons. It is more like a gift.

Notice how often I have used the phrase "at their best" in what I have written here. It is an important qualification. The truth is, no family reflects these characteristics all of the time. A friend once said, "I have heard that studies indicate that 90 percent of families are dysfunctional . . . and I think that is a gross underestimation!" In a way, he was right. Every family is flawed. No family is perfect because all are made up of imperfect people. In fact, most of our deepest hurts are caused by family members. When people come to me in my role as a pastor to discuss something that is troubling them, most often they want to talk about some hurt or conflict that involves a family member. Often the wounds inflicted by family members are both deep and lasting. This shouldn't be surprising. Family members know each other so well, certainly well enough to know just how to hurt one another, especially at such close range!

Within all families hurt is inevitable, so forgiveness is necessary. For families to reflect any of the valuable qualities I have described in this letter, forgiveness must be offered and received on a regular basis, an expected part of what it is to be in a family, like sharing meals together. Like most difficult things, forgiveness requires a lot of practice. Gratefully, all family relationships, not just the most conflicted, give us ample opportunity to practice forgiveness!

These very characteristics of families at their best are also the reasons why families can be a great place to learn something about God. At their best, families love the ones they are stuck with, which can be a powerful reminder of the love of God who is stuck with us all. At their best, families affirm a common story and share values and yet celebrate the gifts of individuals, like the God who treasures each one and invites us all to take part in the ongoing story of God's interaction with the world. At their best, families are safe havens where we are invited to be who we truly are, which is very close to how Christians have always described what the presence of God has meant in their lives. At their best, families can reflect something like the unconditional love that we experience in God's love for us, a love that is expressed in relentless forgiveness and that invites us to respond with forgiveness of our own.

Add these to all of the reasons why I am so grateful that you and I are bundled together in the same family. I may be stuck with you, and you with me, but I can't imagine being stuck with a son I could love any more than I love you. Here is where you usually protest, "That's corny, Dad." And you know my response already, too: "But corny's good. We like corny." Isn't it great to be a part of a family that has shared stories, in which we know all the lines even before they are spoken?

LOVE, D.

26 · Friends

DEAR LAURA,

After your recent birthday party, I remarked to you about your friends. "You have good friends, who love you a lot." And you love them. At your time of life—early teen years—friends are an especially big part of life. I remember that at that time in my own life, my best friend, Steve, and I would often call each other up on a summer day and say, "What do you want to do today?" Looking back, that seems remarkable on several counts. First, that we had no particular schedule, just a summer's day to live. Second, that we assumed that unless something got in our way (our parent's plans or our chores), we would spend it together because we were friends.

Those were precious days. We spent them playing whiffle ball (we devised our own league, with teams, players, and standings), Monopoly, on our bikes, or shooting baskets. But those days passed. Two things intruded to fill the time we once had for each other and our other friends. One thing that intruded was work. Before long our morning paper routes (taken care of early in the morning) gave way to more time-consuming jobs as lifeguards, or flipping hamburgers, or loading trucks for a moving company. Work meant an end to "What do you want to do today?" and generally cut into the time available for hanging out with friends.

The other intrusion into our carefree days and to the long hours spent with friends was girls. We didn't seem to be as interested in girls, or at least interested in them as early, as they were in us boys. But in time, we began to get interested, to go on dates, and to call someone else up—namely a girl we were attracted to—to ask if she'd like to do something together today.

I suppose that it's been true forever, but in some sense it seems especially true today in our society: friendships compete with work and romantic love and often finish third, sometimes a very distant third.

As my life went on, after your Mom and I were married and had a family of our own, and we were beginning our own careers, there was hardly any time, and often precious little energy, left over for friendships. At that time of life, you tend to make friends, those that you do have, through your children. By that I mean that your friends are often people you meet through the sports or school life of your own children.

But that raises some questions. What really is a friend? What's the difference between a friend and an acquaintance? Are the people you work with everyday "friends," or are they colleagues or coworkers? Does a relationship qualify as a friendship if it wouldn't continue when you no longer saw each other at school or work or soccer games?

I am not sure I have answers to these questions. I do think there is a difference between a friend and an acquaintance. But some real friendships are short-lived. Others last, enduring through changes in our lives. Those kinds of friendships are, in my experience, relatively rare.

For many people, the church is a place, a community, where they find and develop friendships that do not depend on common or short-term projects or interests related to your own children or to your work. Even in a society as mobile as ours, people find in the church (as well as some other places) friendships that last through time and changes.

That said, there is a kind of tension—I don't think that's too strong a word—between friendship and Christian faith. That may sound strange, but I think it's true.

What I mean by that is that friendships are, almost by definition, people we chose and who reciprocate by choosing us. Not everyone "clicks" with everyone else. Some people seem to rub us the wrong way (for reasons we may not even understand). With others we just don't find any particular connection. But some we do choose for friends, and they choose us.

Often you realize this quality about friendships—they are relationships we choose—in the absence of such choosing. When, for example, a "friend" chooses someone else to spend time with and not you. Or when you are not as drawn to someone as a friend as they are to you. When these things happen, it can hurt and be difficult. But they signal what is true about friendships. They involve preference. Someone is preferred or chosen. Someone else is not. We have a best friend or a circle of friends, but some are, by definition, left out.

Here's where the tension with Christian faith comes in. Jesus was forever saying things like, "Love your enemies," and "What good is it if you love your friends and do good to them? Why, everyone does that!" "You are to be like your Father in heaven who sends rain on the just and the unjust." In other words, the kind of love Jesus urged was not preferential love, preferring some and not others. It was more universal and unconditional. That, Jesus said, is the way God loves.

Is such indiscriminate love wise? Is it even possible? Can you love everybody? It depends, at least in part, on what you mean by "love." If "love" means liking and having affection for someone, then we probably cannot love everyone. There are some people we just don't like. But if "love" means wanting or seeking the good for another person, then it becomes a real possibility, one that Jesus (and others) lived out. In this sense, you can even love someone that you don't like a whole lot.

So there is a tension between Christian faith and teaching, which emphasize universal love, and the exclusive quality of friendships. Sometimes this tension bubbles up in the life of the church. You may have friends in a church, but you also sense that it's not okay, somehow, to just stick to your friends, or to exclude others.

It is a tension, but not an irreconcilable one. In fact, these two kinds of love—love for friends we have chosen and who have chosen us, and love for all people—are really related. The truest and the deepest friendships help us to grow into and experience a love that is more universal. Such friendships lead us to do things for our friends that are sometimes not in our own best interest. We may, for example, take time away from work or other important things to be with a friend just because they need us. Real friends make real sacrifices to help one another.

When we give or receive this kind of love in a friendship it can point to a love that is more universal and unconditional, to the kind of love that Jesus says God has for all people and that we are to have for all people. A true and deep friendship helps us to love others, all others. Laura, you are a good friend to your friends. I hope that your life will always be blessed by good friendships.

Love, Dad

27 · Siblings

Dear Todd,

People often talk about sibling relationships in ways that suggest that they are the ideal relationships. You might say about someone to whom you feel particularly close, "She is like a sister to me." We speak of "brotherly love." It is often said that the world would be a much better place if we could learn to treat one another "like brothers and sisters." And yet, we don't always get along with our brothers and sisters (I'm sure you've noticed that!). In fact, for many people, their deepest conflicts are with their siblings.

The Bible is brutally honest about human relationships, particularly the ways in which relationships reflect our shortcomings. So it is not surprising that the Bible does not idealize sibling relationships. The very first siblings we encounter in the Bible, in the book of Genesis, are Cain and Abel, the sons of Adam and Eve. From the start, their relationship is marked by rivalry and jealousy and it ends with Cain killing Abel! Later in Genesis we read about other sibling relationships that are far from ideal. We are told that Jacob and Esau didn't even wait to be born before they began to fight; as twins they wrestled in their mother's womb. And it didn't get any better as they grew up. Jacob cheated Esau, and Esau responded by plotting to kill Jacob. Jacob's son, Joseph, was sold into slavery by his brothers because they concluded that Joseph thought too highly of himself. After reading stories like that, one might think it very poor advice indeed to tell someone to treat another person like a brother!

Your relationship with Alanna has been relatively free of conflict almost since the beginning. I say "almost since the beginning" because when you were born Alanna was only two and a half. When we brought you home from the hospital she almost immediately came down with a bad case of hives. It is a classic sign of stress, and it's telling that that is the only time she ever had that uncomfortable skin condition. Then, a few weeks later, while you were sunning yourself in front of the big picture window in the den, she "accidentally" stepped on you. We ran to your aid, of course. In such a circumstance our first concern was for your well-being. In another way, however, we also felt for Alanna. It's hard to make room for a little brother, when you are used to being the sole object of attention and affection. As a parent you know that love given to one child is not taken away from another, that you love each one as if he or she is the only one, but we also know that it doesn't always feel that way when you are the child (after all, we have siblings ourselves!).

I am convinced that our relationships with our siblings can have a profound impact on us. Often it is in relationship to our siblings that we discover and forge our identities as individuals. Even before we try to establish our independence from our parents, we try to differentiate ourselves from our siblings. I think that's one reason why siblings can be so different from one another. When the first child comes along she has certain personality traits and, when the second child comes along, he has to choose from what is left, just as if they are choosing different cards from the same deck.

It is always interesting to see the different ways that siblings reflect or respond to a common heritage. They may share common parents and have lived in the same house, but some siblings seem as different from one another as they would if they had been thrown together by chance.

Wherever those differences come from, they can be very real, and often they are a source of conflict. Many people have their most bitter conflicts with those they are closest to, and for many people that is their brother or sister. It may not be coincidence, then, that Jesus said we should love our neighbors and he also said we should love our enemies, because often they are the same people! That neighbor that Jesus calls you to love as yourself might live as close as the next room and be the one with whom you have to share a bathroom.

Our siblings are important to us for that reason as well. They usually provide our first experience of getting along with someone who is different from us. Parents cannot make their children like one another, but they can (and often do) insist that their children treat one another in a loving manner. When Jesus speaks of loving one's neighbor he seems quite uninterested in how we feel about the person, but he is keenly interested in how we treat the other person. He says that if your neighbor needs a coat, give it to him, and your shirt as well. If she strikes you on the cheek, let her take a wack at your other cheek. Don't wait to feel like doing it (who would ever feel like doing such a thing?), just do it anyway.

Here, as elsewhere, Jesus reverses our expectations. We expect to feel loving before we act lovingly. Jesus tells us to act in a loving manner no matter how we feel. The blessed bonus is that, over time, our actions can be filled with meaning. Our loving actions can become infused with the feelings we associate with love. But it doesn't always start with feelings; often it starts with actions. That's why parents are always saying things like: "Don't hit your sister!" (or "Don't step on your brother!"), "Apologize to your brother," and "Give your sister half of the ice cream." Through these simple actions we can begin to learn the ways of love.

I have been writing here about some of the challenges of relating to siblings. But siblings also can be a real blessing. They certainly have been in my life. Part of the blessing is that so much is shared: common parents, of course, but also a common history, shared experiences, even inside jokes. Out of a common background a common bond can develop. At their best, sibling relationships can be uniquely close.

You can choose your friends, but that also means that friends come and go. You do not choose your siblings, but there is constancy that results from that very lack of choice. You can say of someone, "He is not my friend anymore." You will never be able to say about Alanna, "She is not my sister anymore." I think that is why brotherly/sisterly love is often held up as an ideal. It means that it is the kind of love that cannot turn away. What a wonderful thing to say of any relationship! There is something about the constancy over time in that kind of relationship that can be a real blessing. This seems particularly true to me as I get older, after so many relationships have come and gone.

So I am grateful that you and Alanna have one another. Aside from the time she stepped on you, and in spite of the ways you occasionally still do step on each other's toes, you have been great siblings for one another. My hope is that you have learned, and will continue to learn, something about how to treat others as brothers and sisters through the ways in which you relate to one another.

Love, D.

28 · Parents

Dear Laura,

Maybe you have noticed the picture that sits on the shelf above my desk at home? It shows my Dad and me sitting on a grassy little slope outside the home where I grew up. My father's legs are drawn up, his knees apart, and his arms gently looped over his knees. His left hand is clasped to his right wrist.

I sit next to him, at his right. I am probably eight years old or so. I appear to be trying to emulate his pose, but I am not quite getting it. My knees are too close together, and my arms too far extended. He looks relaxed and at ease. I look bunched and a little uncomfortable. Still there we are. Father and son; parent and child. At one and the same time, the same and yet different. That seems to be the way it is between most parents and children. We are similar, often in surprising ways, and we are different.

Not long ago a book came out about parents and children that got quite a bit of notice. The author claimed that parents and how they raise their children do not really have all much influence on their children's lives or on the kind of adults their children eventually become. According to the author, who had studied many people and families, a person's peers have more influence than a person's parents. Despite her studies, I tend to doubt this claim.

My own experience, and my observation of others, leads me to think that the influence of parents is major. That much is clear. Parents are a major influence in their children's lives. What's a good deal less clear, is how that influence gets translated from parent to child. What's sometimes quite unclear is just how parents have whatever effect they do on their children. There's a lot of mystery about that.

If my own experience and observation are any kind of guide, some children emulate their parents, trying, and sometimes succeeding, to follow in their parent's footsteps. Other children define themselves not by trying to be like their parents, but by trying to be unlike, different from, their parents. Most children do some of both—emulating their parents, and resisting them. Lucky the daughter or son who has parents worthy of emulation, and whose parents are also secure enough to withstand resistance and even, at times, rejection!

The Bible itself reflects this mixed response. The Old Testament tends to lean toward the emulation and respect side. The New Testament (especially Jesus) is more challenging and discordant when it comes to the bonds between parents and children.

The most famous Old Testament teaching on the subject is the fifth of the Ten Commandments: "Honor your father and your mother, that your days may be long in the land which the Lord your God gives you" (Ex. 20:12). "Honor" means to grant respect, esteem, or reverence. It doesn't say "like" your parents. We don't always. Nor does it say what we might expect that it would, that is, "obey" your parents. No, it says "honor."

I take that to mean that we are to grant our parents a special place in our own lives. More than that, we are to grant them our esteem and respect because they have, in some measure, however imperfectly, given their own lives to and for our life.

Of course, some parents do a better job of it than others. Some parents have done terrible things to their own children, hurting or abusing them. But these are the exceptions. Most parents have sacrificed in all sorts of ways for their children. The Old Testament has it right. It is right and good to honor our parents. Such sacrifices, and those who have made them, deserve to be honored.

At the same time, I'm glad that Jesus introduces a different note. He does this consistently enough and often enough that it can't be dismissed as an isolated incident. As young as twelve, Jesus gave his own parents the slip during a family trip to Jerusalem. When they eventually found him he was talking with the teachers and elders in the Temple.

I am sure they were worried and asked him how come he took off. He said, "Did you not know that I must be about my Father's (meaning God's) business?" He is saying that he has other fish to fry, and that there is a higher claim on his life than that of his own parents. Most people will experience times, and should, when a higher claim or authority than that of their parents is made on their lives. We are to honor our parents, but we are to obey God.

Later on, when Jesus is an adult and engaged in his ministry, his mother and brothers showed up one day while he was teaching. They tried to get him to go home with them. He rejected their concern and said to them, and to the crowd who was listening, "Who are my mother and my brothers? Whoever does the will of God is my mother, my brother, and my sister." It was probably a little hard on Jesus' mother and his family to hear him say this, but again family loyalty is given a second or lesser place to God and God's will by Jesus.

This charts a course between twin dangers for parents and children. On one hand, parents do need to be taken seriously and given honor and respect. They care about their children and usually have wisdom and experience from which their children will benefit. On the other, parents too are human beings, with their own particular foibles and blind spots. Take them seriously, but not too seriously. Your parents are not God. Only God is God.

This is good news for parents as well as for their children. Parents too need grace and forgiveness, including the forgiveness of their children. We parents love our children. Most parents would give their own lives for their children's life without a second thought. But we parents are imperfect. We too make mistakes. We are better off not trying to occupy the place in our children's lives that belongs to God and God alone. We both bless and fail our children, as our own parents have blessed and failed us.

Honor your parents, but do not put them on a pedestal. Receive what they have given and will give you, and go on to shape your own life and to be responsible for it.

Love, Dad

29 · Sex

Dear Todd,

Today a friend asked me what I have planned for the day and I told him that, among other things, I was going to write a letter to my son about sex. He replied, "You mean you haven't had 'that talk' with him yet?" He was joking—or, at least, I think he was—so I just said, in a kidding way, "Sure, but that conversation was so much fun, I thought I'd go over it all again." What was revealed by that exchange, even amid the joking, is the implication that sex is the kind of topic that can be covered in a single conversation. A conversation about sex that could be described as "that talk" usually deals with the biology and mechanics of sex. But sex is so much more than that. The straight facts about sex may be simple enough. You learned them quite a number of years ago, now. What sex means and how it relates to the rest of our lives is more complex, however, and, in the long run, more interesting and important, as well.

Another friend of mine says that sex is like nitroglycerin—it can be used either to blow up bridges or heal hearts. I like that image. Growing up I somehow got the impression that the Christian faith had a rather negative view of sex. What I heard was mostly about the dangers, and not so much about the blessings, of sex. My friend's image communicates that sex has great power, but that power is neither good nor bad in itself. It all depends on whether people engage in sex in ways that are destructive or creative, hurtful or healing.

The Christian faith has a lot to say about sex because it is concerned with our entire lives. There are some religions that focus on the part of life that is thought of as "spiritual," but not the Christian religion. The Christian faith is not interested in our spiritual lives, but in our entire lives. It is about our lives as whole persons. Our lives cannot be divided into isolated compartments labeled: body, heart, mind, soul. Those dimensions of our lives are inseparable, so intricately and completely interwoven that we cannot talk about one without talking about the others. It is significant that God did not come to us in some purely spiritual form, but rather in the person, the bodily presence, of Jesus. God came to us in bodily form, which means, in part, that our bodies matter. More important still, in Jesus God took on all the dimensions of human life because our whole lives matter.

Sex has always been a powerful force in human life, but today it seems to be everywhere. That's because sex sells. That is not a new discovery, but these days someone is always trying to sell us something, so sex is ever-present—in advertising, in television and movies, and now on the Internet. And sex is not endlessly interesting, so the depictions of sex become all the more daring and explicit just to keep people's attention. The result is a culture that is simply overheated in the sex department.

One reason—surely not the most important reason, but worth mentioning all the same—that such saturation in sex is unfortunate is that it just isn't very sexy. I remember my reaction when, as a young teenager, I heard that a nude beach opened near the place we went each summer. Naturally, I couldn't wait to check it out. Or, to be more accurate, I couldn't wait to check out the girls. After all, I had already spent quite a bit of time imagining girls without clothes and now they were going to be there in all their naked glory. And, to be honest, the first time or two that my buddies and I walked down to that part of the beach, it was quite exciting. After a time, however, the sights were much less thrilling. The more accessible all of those naked bodies were, the less interesting they became. I even came to appreciate clothes, not just for the way they hide bodies that aren't perfect (which describes all bodies), but also for the way clothes both hide and reveal, which in the long run is much sexier than stark nakedness. I am not the only one who has noticed this. A few years ago a young woman wrote a widely read book praising the benefits of modesty and sexual restraint. One of her points was that modesty is sexier than rampant, unrestrained sexuality. I think she's right.

I grew up in the midst of what was called "the sexual revolution," a time when many people were claiming freedom from the sexual mores that had been in place for generations. Many more people had sex before marriage than was true in our parents' generation, and so it became common for people to have a series of partners. None of that seems too revolutionary today, in part because attitudes toward sex still seem to be changing. Many in my generation questioned why sex should be reserved for a single relationship—marriage—but many people today seem to separate sex from any kind of relationship at all. For many it has become a form of recreation, and sometimes little more.

What is striking to me about the sexual freedom of recent generations is how little people seem to be enjoying their freedom. I have noticed that people who have many sexual partners are very often the ones who are most miserable. To be sure, sex is something to be enjoyed, but when sex is pursued for the sake of enjoyment, the enjoyment itself can disappear.

Perhaps casual sex would not be a problem if we could engage in it without dragging the rest of our selves—mind, heart, and soul, the whole indivisible package—into the encounter. But we cannot. We cannot say to another person, "I am interested in your body; kindly leave your soul outside." Even the suggestion makes the other person feel "used" (it's a telling expression: used like a car is used or a handkerchief is used). And, finally, it isn't possible anyway. You do not have a body as much as you are a body. We are whole people. Any attempt to divide another human being into component parts cannot help but lead to exploitation and hurt.

So sex is not just something we do with our bodies, but with our whole beings. We relate to other people with our whole beings in a variety of ways. Through sex, however, we give ourselves completely to another with every part of our being. In my opening words at a wedding service I refer to marriage as a "union of heart, mind, and body." (I've noticed that everyone gets very quiet at that point in the service. Is it because the minister just referred to sex in church, or because they are aware of how momentous the affirmation is? Perhaps both.) I am convinced that this is one of the reasons why sex is best reserved for marriage.

I suppose this might sound easy for me to say at this point in my life, now that I am married and my hormones don't run as rampant as the bulls of Pamplona. But some things do seem clear to me from this vantage point. In sex we give our whole person to another whole person. That's part of why sex is so powerful and also why it can make us feel uniquely vulnerable. We need a strong, promise-bound, God-sanctioned-and-supported relationship in which to experience that kind of vulnerability.

I gather that the Dutch have a slang term for sex, which is also the word for sewing. In sex two people are sewn together, thread by thread, until they are joined together as one. I suppose we could have sex with many people, but we cannot give ourselves in that whole and complete way to more than one person.

Those who led the "sexual revolution" did so in the name of freedom. But I am convinced that the most complete sexual freedom can only be experienced in marriage. In such a relationship two people can be free to be vulnerable with the other; free to be playful and tender; free from having to perform or pretend; free to enjoy sex within the richest possible context of shared lives; free to entertain the possibility of children; free to give their whole selves completely to the other and to enjoy the other wholly and completely as well.

Sex is not something that is so great that it is worth pursuing in itself, and there are even dangers in doing so. But sex can be a wonderfully blessed, free (not to mention fun!) way to share your life—your whole self—with your lifelong partner. I am grateful that God has such a gift waiting for you.

LOVE, D.

30 · Marriage

Dear Laura,

Apart from Sunday morning worship services, the kind of worship service you have seen me lead more often than any other is a wedding service. I often wonder what you think about as you sit at a wedding.

While this may change, I suspect that what you notice is how beautiful the bride is, dressed in a flowing gown and coming down the aisle. You see how the bride and groom take center stage, so to speak, and then continue as the center of attention and joy at the party that usually follows the service.

Maybe you picture yourself as a bride some day in the future. I know I do. I can't imagine that there will ever be a more beautiful bride than you will be!

There are many people who would say that the beauty and pageantry of a wedding service bear almost no relation to the true reality of marriage. They probably have a point! A wedding service appeals to all sorts of fantasies, and can almost seem like something out of fairy tale. On the other hand, the day-to-day reality of marriage is sharing a bathroom, balancing the checkbook, fixing meals and eating together, laundry and ironing, and maybe, in time, changing diapers and feeding children of your own.

When your Mom and I were married, we had a lovely service in your grandparent's home in Honolulu. It was great fun, and we raced off afterwards for our honeymoon on Kauai. But on Kauai I insisted on riding bikes, instead of renting a car. The result was that within twenty-four hours we were sore from riding old clunker bikes and I as red as a lobster. The fun and festivity had vanished like air from a balloon! Marriage is like that. Ups and downs, the sublime and the sunburns, often in very close proximity!

Still, if we pay attention to the wedding service it does disclose some important things about marriage. For openers, there are usually lots of other people at a wedding besides the bride and the groom. There is family and there are friends. This is important, because when you marry you don't just get one person, you get the whole kit-and-kaboodle.

You may or may not want that, but you get it all the same. You get it in that you'll probably spend lots of time with each other's families over the years. But even if you don't, your husband's family will still be there with you because it's so much a part of who he is, just as our family will prove to be a big part of who you are and how you do things. So that's one thing the wedding service can teach us: it's never "just the two of us." And that's true on the front end and the back end. That is to say, when we marry, who we are has a lot to do with other people and how they have affected us, often in ways we don't even know. And it's also true in the other direction as well: our marriage will shape and have an effect on others, children if we have them, but others too.

Maybe you've noticed that wedding services are not usually very long, maybe thirty or forty minutes altogether. Given the months of preparation and planning, that often strikes me as odd. But when you get right down to it, there's not a whole lot to a wedding. Some readings, a little music, a short sermon, and a prayer or two. The heart of it all is so brief that you could miss it altogether if you felt the urge to sneeze and had to run out to get a tissue.

The heart of it is the marriage vow. A vow is a promise by which a person binds him or herself. It's a string of words two people use to tie their lives together, and after those words are spoken nothing is ever the same again. While the exact words of the vow may vary some, most go about like this: "(Name of your husband/ wife to be), I give myself to you to be your wife (husband). I promise to love and sustain you in the covenant of marriage from this day forward, in sickness and health, in plenty and want, in joy and in sorrow, so long as we both shall live."

One of the things I often notice during weddings is how nervous people are. They start breathing very rapidly. Their hands shake. They feel faint or wobbly, and sometimes start to giggle uncontrollably. At times like this I will say, "Now, just take a few, slow, deep breaths," and they look back at me as if I had said the most inspired and helpful thing they have heard in their entire lives. My theory is that even if our minds do not plumb the depths of what is happening, our bodies are telling us, "This is big." And it is. We are giving our word. Pledging our lives.

What are we pledging our lives to? What is this thing called marriage, and what is its purpose? The purpose of marriage is deceptively simple. It is to share life together. I say "deceptively" because while that sounds simple enough, sharing life with another person for a lifetime is in reality anything but simple. Trust me on this one, it is complex stuff. Your mother and I have been married over thirty years. It has been, and continues to be, both a wonderful blessing and a great challenge.

You would think that after thirty years you would know everything there is to be known about another person. You don't. There is always more to learn, as well as new experiences to be encountered and shared together. But that is also the great beauty and power of marriage, the intimate sharing of life with another through time and change. It takes time. A lifetime is about right.

What about divorce? What happens when the promises we make in the wedding service are broken? The truth is that we all break that promise. Few, if any, married people "love and sustain each other" without failure or hurt. A marriage, if it is to survive, requires frequent and generous doses of forgiveness.

But, as you know, many marriages (about half, if the statistics are to be trusted) end in divorce. Like many people, I find it difficult to say that the end of a particular marriage is right or wrong, good or bad. But I am sure of this: it is always sad. Sad and full of pain. Some people conclude that it will bring more sadness and pain to stay together than to separate. Because few of us know what it is like inside someone else's marriage, I am inclined to take their word for it.*

But I also know that some people who run from their marriages are really running away from themselves, and that hardly ever works, for obvious reasons. Moreover, when that is the case, people leave a lot of deeply hurt and bewildered people behind them.

Marriage is, among other things, a way we come to know ourselves. We discover, in sharing life together over time, our own strengths and weaknesses, our own capacity to love and forgive, as well as our capacity to hurt and wound. It is not an easy path, but it is a reliable one. It is a path that entails suffering, because there is no love apart from suffering. But it is also a path that entails joy, the joy that comes from knowing another and from being deeply and truly known.

LOVE, DAD

*It is true that Jesus speaks disapprovingly of divorce. But he does so in a time and society where only men had legal rights and were able to divorce or dismiss their wives on a whim, without their wives having any say. Jesus condemns this kind of selfishness and treating other people like objects. Sometimes divorce is still like that. But other times, a husband and wife agree that their marriage was a mistake or should not continue, which is a different situation than the one of which Jesus spoke.

Letters about
Difficult Matters

31 · Race and the Church

Dear Laura,

Martin Luther King Jr., whose life and legacy we celebrate every January 15th (or the Monday closest to it), once observed, "Sunday morning at eleven o'clock is the most segregated hour of the week." In other words, when it came to accepting people of other races, the church was no better, and perhaps worse, than any other institution in America.

It was true, in King's time and place (the American South in the 1940s, '50s, and '60s) that there were churches that overtly discriminated against people of color and used the Bible to justify their prejudices. But today, except for some pretty wacko groups and people on the fringe of society, that is no longer the case. And yet, on Sunday morning, with some notable exceptions, people still tend to worship God mostly with people of their own race.

Why? What's going on? Is this a problem?

Not long after many Americans and Christians began to embrace racial equality and integration in the 1950s and 1960s, this movement bumped into a competing value: culture. Culture as in communities of memory, language, history, and tradition. Often these cultures were defined by race or ethnicity. There are Scandinavian American, Japanese American, African American, Filipino American, German American, and lots more, cultures within our society. We are a multicultural society in America.

The churches and other religious institutions not only help people get in touch with God and the sacred, they are also like carriers or stewards of particular ethnic cultures and traditions. Today when Japanese Americans worship with other Japanese Americans, European Americans with European Americans, or African Americans with African Americans, it has less to do with racial prejudice than it does with sharing a particular history, set of traditions, and cultural experience.

In our society where these kinds of communities of memory and tradition are always being undermined by mobility and by commercialism, the church has become a primary caretaker of such cultures and their traditions. In other words, at just about the time that Americans and Christians were ready to embrace Martin Luther King's words that "A person should be judged by the content of his character, not the color of his skin," we also got very interested in our different cultural backgrounds and traditions. Funny how these things happen!

The rub, so to speak, is not between something that is clearly bad (racial prejudice) and something that is clearly good (racial equality and acceptance). It is, as is often the case in life, between two competing good things. In this case, racial equality and acceptance compete with ethnic and cultural identity and tradition. Is the fact that churches so often are carriers and caretakers of ethnic and cultural traditions, and therefore mostly one racial group or another, a good thing or a bad thing?

Probably it is some of both. Personally, I value the different ethnic and cultural traditions that make up the United States. I do understand too that often when majority groups say to a minority group, "Come on over to our church and join us," what that means is, "Give up your own ways and traditions and accept ours." That doesn't seem quite fair.

At the same time, I am sad, in a way, that the church, and our society as a whole, has not been more successful at living out Martin Luther King's dream, and the ideas of a racially integrated society and church. I am sad that the churches are not full of people of all different races worshipping together.

I grew up in Arlington, Virginia, a suburb of Washington, D.C., and a neighboring town to Alexandria, Virginia, the community featured in the movie *Remember the Titans* that we saw together recently. That movie, as you recall, tells the story of the integration of the schools through the story of a football team and the experience of its coaches and players. Our schools in Arlington were integrated as I began eighth grade. We had high hopes that a new era was beginning. In some ways it did. But in other ways it did not.

But even before school integration came, my church had involved me in getting to know kids of different races. I went to racially integrated youth camps and conferences, which doesn't seem like any big deal now but it sure was then. Anyhow, I have the church to thank for my first experiences of getting to know people of other races. Besides being a vocal supporter of integration and an end to prejudice, the church in which I grew up even picketed the local movie theaters to protest their policies that had whites sit on the main floor and blacks in the balcony of the theater.

I also remember the summer night in 1964 when I was at a church camp with black and white boys and girls. That day President Lyndon Johnson signed the Civil Rights Act, a critical step in overcoming racial segregation and the laws that had supported it. We celebrated the Civil Rights Act that night as if the Kingdom of God itself had come. We were, we believed, at the beginning of a whole new era and a new society. In some ways that new society has come. In many ways it has not.

It is interesting to contrast my experience growing up with your mother's. She grew up in Hawaii, where people of different races mingled and shared things much more freely than was true in the American South and East where I grew up. Hawaii was the one state where no racial group was in the majority. That will become true in many other parts of the United States in your lifetime.

For me, the church has continued to play an important role in reaching across racial barriers. As a minister, I have served two congregations that were multiracial in their makeup. Today our church, as you know, has joined in a partnership with a large African American, Baptist congregation. And our congregation has been involved recently in starting a new, multiracial, multicultural congregation in south Seattle.

But still these are the exceptions that prove the rule. Even in Hawaii, where I served a multiracial church in the 1980s, most of the churches there have remained one ethnic or racial group or another.

In many ways, the new society has not come. Is this likely to change? I think it is. One thing I've become aware of in writing these letters to you is just how much has actually changed since I was your age. Some change, of course, is not for the good. But still, change does take place. Tremendous social changes have taken place in the not-quite-forty years since I was your age.

While there is still lots of racial and ethnic division in our country, some of it by choice and some of it because of prejudice, I agree with a man I heard speak recently, a Mexican American, who said, "We are all becoming brown." He meant that, racially and ethnically, we are all slowly getting mixed up and mixed in because people keep falling in love with people of other races and cultures. You know what a marvelous blend of races and cultures you are. From my family there is Irish, English, and some Scottish. From your mother's there is Mexican and Czech. Chances are there is more than these and we just don't know about it.

Race and culture are important, but probably not as important as we have made them in America today. That man I mentioned said, "I am you, and you are me, and we are all becoming brown." At some level our separateness is an illusion. At its best the church has known that and helped us to act on that knowledge. It will be fascinating to see how these issues play out in your lifetime.

Love, Dad

32 · Money and Wealth

DEAR TODD,

People are sometimes surprised to learn that Jesus talked more about money than he talked about anything else, except the Kingdom of God. Most people assume that Jesus would be more interested in subjects that are considered more "spiritual" than money. Let this surprise you, as well: Jesus talked more about money than he talked about love. He talked more about money than he talked about helping others. He talked more about money than he talked about how we are to serve God. That would be shocking, indeed, except that when Jesus talked about money, he was talking about all of those things. How we understand and use money has a great deal to do with how we express love, help others, and serve God.

Jesus was always down-to-earth about such matters. Come to think of it, that is not a bad description of Jesus: a down-to-earth God. He did not stay in some heavenly sphere, but rather showed us how we are to find God and serve God in the very earthly places in which we live each day. So Jesus talked about money a great deal because how we understand and use money is an important spiritual matter. He recognized that money is a powerful force in our lives. That is, he concerned himself with money, not because it shouldn't mean anything to us, but because it does.

People sometimes quote the expression "money is the root of all evil" as if it were merely an old proverb. Actually, that expression is a misquote of the biblical passage that reads, "Love of money is the root of all evil" (1 Tim. 6:10). Notice the difference: according to the Bible, money itself is not evil. Money is neutral. It can be used for good or ill. Our attitude toward money can be faithful or sinful. Which means that there is a great deal at stake in how we use and understand money!

There are a number of dangers associated with money. For one, there is the gap between the rich and poor, which raises questions of justice. And, make no mistake, they are difficult questions, questions that cause us to examine how we live. For instance: Does God intend for me to eat more food than I need, while there are those who do not have enough food to live? Should we have a second home where we can gather as a family, even when there are families who cannot afford any home of their own? Is it right for you to play soccer on a sunny suburban field with a ball made by someone your own age in another country for just pennies an hour?

These questions become all the more pressing because, in our time, the gap between the "haves" and the "have-nots" has widened to the dimensions of a great canyon. In many ways, money separates us. It poses danger to our relationships.

Recently I was asked to convene a meeting that happened to include people from a variety of circumstances, some who have more money and others who have considerably less—that is, people from both sides of the canyon. I was eager to convene this meeting, but it took me a while to figure out where it should take place. Normally, such a gathering would take place at our home, but I wasn't entirely comfortable with that. As you know, our house is not at all lavish by the standards of our community, but surely it would appear so to some of our guests who live elsewhere. Then I began to ask myself: if I am self-conscious about having all of this stuff, should I have it at all? It is a disturbing—and important—question to ask. So we did have the meeting at our house. I concluded that my discomfort was not to be avoided because it arose out of my reluctance to look into the eyes of these good folk and, at the same time, to recognize the chasm that threatens to divide us. In the end, we cannot choose to ignore economic divisions between people, even as we dare not get used to such divisions.

Our love of money can also result in danger to our environment. We consume so much, particularly in relation to people in other parts of the world, and in ways that cannot be sustained. One of the things you and I have in common is a distaste for the job of sorting our trash and recyclables and taking it all to the dump. There is only one thing I appreciate about that chore: as I wade through all of the boxes that once contained items we bought, all the empty cans and jars left from the foods we have consumed, the piles of glossy catalogues of things we do not need and only vaguely want, I confront again the unsettling truth that all of our consumption puts a burden on our environment. Then, when I take it all to the dump and see our large piles added to the enormous mounds of stuff from other households, I often wonder: perhaps individual families can "afford" all of this consumption, but can our world?

Even if poverty were eliminated, and even if the earth's environment were not threatened, our love of money can still be dangerous to our souls. Quite simply, it can distract us from those things that are most important. All of our focus on money, the harried and frantic getting and spending that so occupies us, can distract from those things that contribute to a truly rich and fulfilling life. I have in mind things like spending time with family or friends, developing a relationship with God, enjoying the gifts of nature, even pursuing some interest or hobby. The love of money can threaten all of those things, and often does. When we spend money we are called consumers, but often what is being consumed is our own lives.

People will sometimes say that they only want enough money that they won't have to worry about it. But such an amount of money does not exist. In some ways the rich worry about money as much as the poor do. They worry about losing their money and about how they will maintain all of their stuff. Or, as someone I know put it, "We are afraid of losing what is already killing us." I have concluded that the best way to be relatively free from worry about money is not to have more, but to need less.

Money can keep us at a distance from God in one other way: often the more we have, the less likely we are to thank God for all we have. It is the rich who are tempted to boast that they are "self-made." So when the cartoon character Bart Simpson offered a prayer before a family meal, he said, "Dear God, we bought all of this stuff with our own money, so thanks for nothing."

Contrary to our friend Bart, Christians are asked to understand that what we call "our" possessions and "our" money is not ours. Everything we have comes from God and in a very real way still belongs to God. We come into the world without possessions and we leave the same way. In between, we "have" possessions, including money, as if on loan. We are not owners, the masters of all we possess. Rather, we are God's caretakers of what has been entrusted to us for a time.

What would it mean to live out that understanding? If all of our possessions are on loan from God, if we did not earn them and do not deserve them, then when we share with those who have less, we are sharing something that was never really ours in the first place. We are merely acting out the understanding that everything in life is God's. And when we work against the great disparity of wealth in our world, we are expressing the understanding that God's love and God's blessings are not given on the basis of merit, but freely to all. If the natural world itself has been given to us as caretakers, we will tread more lightly on the earth, even as we treat carefully those things that are loaned to us, so that they will be in good shape when we pass them along to others. Perhaps this understanding can also help us love money a little less, so that we are free to love other things all the more.

Todd, I realize that these are challenges worthy of a lifetime. In many ways, I am still trying to live up to them myself. That must be why Jesus talked about money so much. In that area of life, we all need all the help we can get.

LOVE, D.

33 · Abortion

Dear Laura,

This is a tough topic! Throughout my entire adult life there has been no other single issue about which people in our society have been more divided than abortion. Some—called the "pro-life" side—oppose abortion and believe it should be against the law. Others—the "pro-choice" side—believe that women should be free to choose if they will give birth to a child conceived in their womb, or not.

I am old enough to remember when abortion was against the law. When I was in high school we would hear whispered stories of girls who had become pregnant. Some left school for a while, gave birth, and then gave the child up for adoption. Some just became mothers at the age of fifteen, sixteen, or seventeen, and usually dropped out of school as a result. Others who came from families with more money would travel to other countries where abortion was legal and have an abortion there. Still others would go to people who would perform illegal abortions, often in unsanitary and unsafe conditions. Sometimes these young women would be damaged for life or die because of a badly performed abortion.

In 1973, the United States Supreme Court reached a decision ("Roe versus Wade" was the name of the now famous court case) that made abortion legal. Many people believed this was a good thing and a great advance. No longer would there be illegal or unsafe abortions. No longer would some women be forced to give birth to children they did not want or for which they could not care.

Others were horrified by that same Supreme Court decision. The life of an unborn child was, they believed, sacred and should be protected by law. For them abortion was no different than murder. Over time these became the "pro-choice" and "pro-life" sides, and they have been battling ever since.

In some instances, and I believe this is one, there are no perfect solutions, but the best ones lie somewhere in the middle between two opposed positions. My own position would be like that, between these two — maybe pro-life with a lot of flexibility, or pro-choice with limitations.

I do believe that the life of an unborn child is sacred, and that ending that life is a sin. But I also believe that there are circumstances that make that terrible choice the best, if tragic, one.

As a minister I have counseled women and couples who were considering an abortion. It has always been, in these instances, a very, very hard decision. The people I worry about are those for whom it is not a hard decision. Those for whom an abortion is no big deal — I have trouble with that.

One woman, whom I counseled, had after the birth of her first child suffered a very serious and long-lasting depression. It was so bad that she had tried to kill herself and had to be hospitalized. She was terribly afraid that this might happen to her again if she gave birth to the child in her womb. She decided to have an abortion, and as her pastor, I supported her.

In another instance, a couple came to see me who were considering an abortion. Their doctor had informed them that the child in the mother's womb had serious birth defects. He had heart problems, crippled legs, and deformed feet. The doctor had recommended that they have an abortion. The husband in this couple leaned toward an abortion, but the wife was against it. We talked it all over a couple of times, and they eventually decided not to have an abortion. I supported that decision.

When their son was born I was with them at the hospital. He had to have heart surgery soon after he was born. Over the next couple years the little boy had several surgeries for his legs and feet. Today, he is healthy and growing, but he will probably never walk quite normally. He still uses a wheelchair some of the time.

The point of sharing these two stories with you is to say that the decision to have an abortion, or not, is often a very difficult and complex decision. The law is a pretty blunt instrument for making such difficult and complex decisions. For that reason, I have favored the pro-choice position. When abortion is a legal option it allows women and couples to arrive at their own best decision given their particular circumstances.

At the same time, I am uneasy with the pro-choice position, and I wonder if I have come to the right decision. One of the reasons I am uneasy is that for too many people the decision to have an abortion is not hard enough. It is but another form of birth control. "Having a child doesn't fit in with my life right now, so I'll have an abortion." It's not, or shouldn't be, that simple. Having a child, or not having one, is not like having a parakeet.

It is not only that for some people the life of a child and an abortion is taken too lightly, it is also that some will, because abortion is legal and available, feel pushed in a way to do that. They will feel "forced" to have an abortion in somewhat the same way that before 1973 others were "forced" to bear a child.

I don't know if that makes sense to you? What I am trying to say is that sometimes people make a certain choice because they can and because it looks like the easiest way out. (I have the same doubts about euthanasia, that is, allowing people who are sick to choose to be put to death in order to avoid suffering. I am afraid that people who are in that position may feel "forced," in an odd way, to choose euthanasia, not so much for their own good, but to spare their families the suffering or expense of their illness.)

So I struggle with abortion and whether I've made the right decision about it.

There's one further thought I have. Sometimes people can be helped to avoid an abortion they don't really want if they have support from others. That support may be a good way to let the child be adopted. Or it may be support to raise their child themselves. This is another place, besides helping people to reach a decision, where the Church comes in.

One of the reasons that some, perhaps many, women choose abortion is because they are alone. The man who fathered the child is not a husband and cannot be counted upon to be a good father. They have little in the way of family or other community support.

Sometimes when this is the situation, people turn to the Church for help in raising their children. In the Church they find surrogate grandparents, aunts, and uncles. Sometimes they find practical aid, as the Church helps a mother or couple to find an apartment or a job. My point is that too often people chose an abortion because they don't have a real family or community of people that care about them. So abortion is, in a way, a reflection on all of us.

But sometimes the Church is that family and that community, and I rejoice in that.

The Church is often at its best, in fact, when its helps us to make room in our lives for the unexpected. The unexpected may be a stranger that we are able to welcome because the Church has taught us to welcome the stranger. The unexpected may be an accident that leaves a person disabled. The Church helps that person to realize that, despite the accident, his or her life is not over. Sometimes the unexpected is a death. Then, too, the Church helps those who survive, to go on after the death of a loved one. And sometimes the unexpected is a birth, a baby. Then too, the Church helps people to live with the unexpected. Faith in God and the support and care of the Church often helps people to cope with the unexpected and to become better people for it.

Love, Dad

34 · Homosexuality

DEAR LAURA,

Like abortion, homosexuality has been a hot, and divisive, issue in our society and in the church during most of my adult lifetime. Unlike abortion, however, homosexuality is specifically addressed in the Bible. There are four clear references to homosexual behavior, two in the Old Testament and two more in the New Testament. All four condemn sexual activity between persons of the same gender.

Given this, how did our congregation, along with many others in the United Church of Christ, as well as some in other denominations, come to the conclusion that gay and lesbian persons are welcome as full partners and participants in the church and Christian life? The answer to that question provides a good example of how different people and churches interpret the Bible and the teachings of their faith in different ways.

As I've said, the Bible, where it speaks directly of homosexual behavior, does condemn it. It is important to note, however, where and how these references occur in the Bible. In the New Testament, both times that homosexual behavior is mentioned occur in the letters of Paul. And to be fair, you would have to say that Paul only mentions it in passing. In the Gospels and the words of Jesus there is no mention of homosexuality at all. I remember an older minister who was asked by members of his congregation why he didn't have more to say about homosexuality. He replied that he had as much to say on the subject as Jesus himself did, which was precisely nothing!

The point is that some parts of Scripture are to be taken more seriously, or weighted more heavily, than other parts. Think of it this way. Say you have a friend who has certain qualities and characteristics that are central to who she is, that are the core of her personality and way of living. You will take these central themes more seriously than you might take an occasional or offhand remark.

It is somewhat the same with the Bible. We ought to take its major themes and priorities as more important than occasional or offhand remarks. We ought to take some parts of the Bible, and some teachings of the Church, more seriously than other ones. For example, the Gospels are more important, I believe, than, say, the Letters of Peter in the New Testament. They are more at the heart of it all. In the Old Testament, the Book of Exodus is more important than the Book of Habakkuk, though I personally love Habakkuk!

When you look at the central themes of Jesus' life and teaching one of the clearest is God's love and acceptance for outsiders, for the persons others think suspect or bad because they are different from the majority. Jesus was constantly in the company of such outcasts, some who were cast out because of an illness, others because they were the wrong ethnicity, and others because they had somehow failed in life. By his actions Jesus said, "God doesn't see things exactly the way we human beings do."

There is no doubt, when you look at history and even society today, that people who are homosexual have been excluded, mistreated, and even killed, for no other reason than that they were different from the majority and by their existence challenged the norms of the majority. On the topic of homosexuality, if you take the major and consistent themes of the Bible, rather than the minor and occasional ones, as your basis, you come out in one of two places. Either you have to say what the minister I mentioned above said, which is not much, or you have to say that God takes the side of the outcast and those who are in trouble, which in our times often includes persons who are homosexual.

That's one point about interpreting the Bible and the teachings of the Church that is important beyond just this issue: try to see the forest and not only the individual trees.

Here's a second point about interpreting the Bible that is illustrated by the debate over homosexuality. While human nature remains much the same throughout history, the historical conditions in which people live their lives do change, as does our knowledge and information. Because human nature remains much the same, the Bible, though it was written in vastly different times and cultures than our own, remains relevant. But because historical conditions and information changes, you have to be aware of this as you read and interpret the Bible.

For example, in many ancient societies, including the one described in parts of the Old Testament, it was not unusual for a man to have more than one wife. This was probably a way of being sure to have children in a time when your children were your source of security in your old age. Today things have changed and this is no longer accepted. The fact that having multiple wives is mentioned doesn't mean the Bible is supporting it or should properly be used to support men having more than one wife. It was just part of that culture.

Here's my point as it pertains to the matter at hand, homosexuality. The few biblical writers who mention homosexual behavior seem to be of their time in believing that everyone, all men and women, were by nature heterosexual, or attracted to persons of the opposite sex. For someone to have homosexual relationships was then, by definition, to distort or violate their own nature.

These writers did not ever imagine, I believe, that some people might be, by nature, homosexual, or sexually drawn to persons of their own sex. But both scientific study and my own experience and observation have led me to conclude that a certain portion of any human society is made up of persons whose sexual orientation is toward persons of their own gender. For such folks, it is as natural to be attracted to persons of their own gender or sex as it is for most others to be attracted to persons of the opposite gender. That's a very different perspective than that of the biblical writers who do mention homosexuality, one based on different information.

Rather than condemning and excluding those for whom attraction to persons of their own gender is normal, it seems to me far better that the Church welcome and include such folks, giving them the nurture and support of the Church, especially since life is difficult enough as it is. But just as we encourage heterosexual people to celebrate their sexuality in the context of a committed relationship, and not to use or abuse others sexually, we try to encourage homosexual people to live out their sexuality in a relationship that is mutual, caring, just, and faithful throughout their lives.

This whole matter—how society and the Church think about homosexuality and relate to people who are homosexual—has been a big one in the years of my ministry. I remember that the first church I served, back in the late 1970s, was seriously divided over, at least in part, the issue of whether the church should support full legal rights and protections for homosexual persons. It was hard. Some people left the church, but we maintained our support for the civil rights of gay and lesbian people.

A decade ago Plymouth went through a two-year process of study and discernment, which led to becoming an "Open and Affirming Congregation," that is, one that welcomes gay and lesbian persons and their families. At times this debate was difficult and even painful. In many, even most, churches, it is far from a settled matter. I am glad our church has done this. The study and dialogue was good for us. And our decision was the right thing to do. There are, however, decent and faithful people who have not reached the same conclusion. It is important to respect their convictions, without abandoning one's own, because none of us has the full and complete truth.

Over the years I've known many gay and lesbian people in the Church. Most have been wonderful people and wonderful Christians. But just like any other slice of the population, you cannot, I've found, generalize about gay and lesbian people. You cannot, in other words, say that they are all this way or all that way, any more than you can generalize about heterosexual people. God sees them as God sees all of God's children, as individuals. Individuals with possibilities, problems, potentials, and gifts to give and share with the Church and with the whole human community.

Love, Dad

35 · Gender

DEAR LAURA,

There are two creation stories in the Book of Genesis. In the first, "God created man in his own image, male and female he created them." (Gen. 1:27) In the second, God made the first man to fall into a deep sleep. While he slept, God took a rib from him and fashioned from it a partner suitable for man, woman.

Despite the variation in the two stories, the end result is the same. Human beings come in two basic models, or genders, male and female, man and woman. But what does it mean to be a woman? What does it mean to be a man?

Though the Genesis story, the second one, begins with a man from whom woman is formed, the actual biology of it is pretty much the other way around. We start out, in the womb, female. When a fetus is about two or three weeks old, the hormones kick in that result in some developing the characteristics of a male. Later still, about the ages of twelve to fourteen, boys get another burst of these same hormones, which results not only in things like facial hair, or a beard, but also in a more pronounced (than girls) upper body development (shoulders, arms, chest). Finally, these hormones tend to make boys (and men) more aggressive than girls typically are. Girls and women, on the other hand, receive a different hormonal infusion, leading them to develop the organs necessary to conceive, carry, birth, and feed a child.

It oversimplifies things a good deal, but still it's not inaccurate to say that men, with their greater upper body strength and aggressiveness, tended to become the hunters. Women, with the capacity to carry, birth, and feed children, tended to become the gatherers.

Those are the basics, the biology, of male and female, and the differences between them. What we human beings have made of the biology is another thing again. The differences in bodies and biology of male and female have led to different social roles for men and women. Because of men's greater strength the social roles have often, but not always, favored men. At their best, men have used their generally greater strength and aggressiveness to protect the vulnerable. At their worst, men have used these same characteristics to dominate the vulnerable and to subject them to their own will.

The biological differences between women and men have been a factor in the different social roles they play. But it is not always easy to sort out how much the different roles of women and men are a function of biological difference (what you might call "nature") and how much they are a function of the norms and patterns of a given society ("nurture"). In my lifetime the social roles prescribed for women and men have become less clear and more open to change.

This has happened for many reasons, including the advocacy by many women and some men for change. It also has something to do, I suspect, with social changes that mean that physical strength is less important in the scheme of things than once was true. For example, if you are hunting or farming for a living, physical strength matters more than it does if you are working primarily with your mind or with information.

Nevertheless, social roles tend to take on a life of their own and are not easily changed, especially when change means that some lose power while others gain power. It has been quite a while since most men went out hunting for a family's food, bringing it home for women to prepare. Yet in many families women are still expected to do all the cooking even if they are also working full time outside the home. Good deal for the men! Despite this a lot has changed. From opening doors in the professions—medicine, law, and ministry—to sharing the kitchen and housework, a lot has changed in women's and men's roles in the last forty years in our society.

A great example is women's sports. When I was in high school and college, there were few, if any, sports played by or available to girls and women. Boys played; girls cheered from the sidelines. That changed with the Title IX federal laws in the early 1970s. Title IX made sure girls and women had the same resources and opportunities in sports that boys and men did. It is one of the great laws and changes of the twentieth century. Today there is a growing number of girls and women involved in sports, with a growing number of fans as well.

A flip side to the story of wider opportunity for women is that many men and boys are finding themselves less certain about their own identity and role as men. While the last couple of generations have been concerned about widening opportunity for women and supporting their growth and advancement, it appears to me that at least some boys today are less confident and sure of themselves.

What did Jesus have to say about the roles of women and men? Not much really. I can't think of anywhere that Jesus says "This is what a man is to be and do, and this is what a woman is to be or do." He seems more focused on individuals and on what it means to be a human being.

That said, it is still clear that Jesus shattered many of the conventions and taboos when it came to women and men. Sometimes he did this simply by talking to women, something a rabbi or religious teacher in his time did not do. He also included women in his company and defended women when men tried to put them down. While the twelve apostles were men, it is also clear that women were among the larger group of his disciples or followers. Later, after Jesus, women were among the leaders of churches described in the New Testament.

At the same time, religion has often been one of the institutions that reenforced and maintained society's roles for women and men. Christianity, as a religion, has done this too, even though its founder, Jesus, showed little interest in it himself. There are, you might say, two strands in the Church and Christianity. One has reenforced and maintained the clear and sometimes limiting social roles of men and women. In many instances, women have been accorded a secondary role and excluded from power and decision making in the church. At the same time, however, another, more revolutionary, strand has challenged and sometimes overturned these clearly prescribed roles and limitations. I am proud that our Congregational/ United Church of Christ ordained the first woman to ministry long before other churches. Her name was Antoinette Brown and she was ordained as a minister in 1854, even before women got the right to vote in the United States!

Today there is greater equality between men and women, as there should be. But these changes have also created questions and uncertainty for many people. And that's always a challenge. Are there particular social roles that women should play? That men should have? Are there particular qualities or behaviors that go with one's gender? What does it mean to be a man? What does it mean to be a woman? Generally, people are less sure about how to answer those questions than was true, say, fifty years ago.

Whether that's a bad thing or a good thing depends a lot on your viewpoint and situation. For your Mom and me it has meant that we have had to change and to do more discussion and negotiation than was probably true for our parents or grandparents. Sometimes that's been hard, but we have also learned from it. Certainly part of what it means to be a human being is to be able to adapt to change. Besides, I kind of enjoy housework!

Those hormones and biological differences are still there. It is wise to acknowledge and respect them without allowing them to determine or dictate the opportunities available to girls and boys or men and women. But I would go a step beyond even that. It seems to me that one of the great things about life is that we are male and female, that there is difference. *Viva la difference!* say the French. Should you fall in love with and marry a young man, you will have as your life partner someone who is in a basic way different from you. Personally, I think that's great, that in our most intimate relationships we are bonded with someone who is and always will be different than we are. Learning from our differences, and learning that people are different, seems to me a source of blessing and delight. How boring it would be if we human beings only came in one model!

Love, Dad

36 · Life After Death

Dear Todd,

Most parents seem to be able to remember the time they explained to their children what is sometimes called "the facts of life." At least, I've heard many such stories from parents, mostly humorous stories filled with awkward miscues from the parents and funny misunderstandings from their children. But, to tell you the truth, I don't remember much of what was said or how you responded on that occasion—except, as I recall, your frequent use of the word "yuck."

What I do remember with blazing clarity, however, are the conversations I had with you and Alanna about, not the facts of life, but the facts of death. No one prepared me for those conversations. I never heard stories from other parents about the day that their children learned that one day we die, each of us. I think that's because, in some ways, death is the last taboo, that thing we will not talk about.

I remember very well Alanna's first confrontation with death. She and a little friend of hers encountered a dead frog flattened on the road next to our house. That was difficult enough for Alanna to take, but then her friend told Alanna, "There is nothing to get upset about. Everyone ends up like that . . . you, that frog, your mother, your father, your brother . . ." Alanna responded to that news by running home in tears. I still remember the grief-stricken look on her face. I remember the way I scrambled to find something to say. I remember just how I held her. She cried for hours. One's first encounter with death is never a trifling thing.

I don't remember what occasioned the first conversation you and I had about death. But I do remember how you, like Alanna, wept with great swelling sobs that lasted for a very long time and seemed to come from a depth that had not been tapped before or since. I also remember searching for something to say to you, something that would be both reassuring and true. I remember saying that death is not something to fear, even though I can't tell you exactly what it will be like. I said that God takes care of us in death, even as God takes care of us in life. I tried to assure you that, in some mysterious way we cannot fully imagine, we will live even after we die. My words continued to flow, and so did your tears. Such a huge reality. Such a little boy.

Then, just when I thought you were feeling somewhat comforted, you said, "Yeah, but I won't get to do stuff!" And once you expressed that sense of loss, a new torrent of tears was released.

I think that's the last time we have talked at any length about death. I get the impression that, for the most part, you would rather avoid the subject. Many people—of all ages—react that way. And that's quite understandable. As I say, death is such a huge reality. But, through this letter, I want to continue the conversation because I think there are ways in which our faith has things to say about death that you will appreciate now, things that you could not have been expected to appreciate as a little boy.

The authors of scripture do not try to diminish the power of death by patting us on the head and offering a few easy words of reassurance, the equivalent of "There, there, it really doesn't matter." The Bible does not depict death as friendly, or easily defeated. No, death is a huge reality, so enormous and powerful that only God can overcome it. One of the reasons that Easter is so central to our faith is that, in Jesus' resurrection, a fearsome enemy—death—has been defeated. And that victory was won for all of us. As people who participate in the life of Jesus, we will also die, but death will not be the end of us, either.

But what will this afterlife be like? That question has occupied people of faith for centuries. At the time Jesus lived there were people called "Sadducees" who didn't believe in a life after death, so they pressed him for details about what it will be like. They were trying to trick Jesus into saying something that would demonstrate the absurdity of his teaching. They asked Jesus, "Say that a wife had seven husbands and each of them died, who would be her husband in the afterlife?" That does seem like a thorny problem! In response, Jesus said, in essence, that it's a problem only if we imagine our future life as being just like this life. But the afterlife will be different, unlike anything we have yet experienced. We will live like angels, he said. But how do angels live? No one really knows and we cannot even imagine such a life.

When the Apostle Paul received a question about what the afterlife is like, he responded by offering a helpful comparison. He said that our life on this earth is like a seed of wheat. When we die it is like that seed being buried in the earth. That buried seed will eventually have a new and different life as a shaft of wheat. We cannot know from the seed alone what wheat will be like. If all we knew were seeds, if we had never seen a field of wheat, our imaginations could not help us anticipate what wheat looks like. If we ourselves were seeds, we could not possibly imagine what it would be like to live as wheat. We could no more understand the nature of this new life than an unborn child could anticipate what life is like outside the mother's womb.

So we are offered no details. But this seems clear: scripture is more concerned with *who*, rather than *what* is beyond the grave. On this the New Testament accounts speak with conviction and in unison: when we die, we die into the eternal presence of God. To be sure, we can experience the presence of God in glimpses and intimations during our earthly lives. After we die, however, we will experience God in a sure and immediate way that is different from anything we have experienced in this life. The God who accompanied us in this life, whose presence we may have sensed along the way, this same God will greet us in the next life and we will know God in an unmistakable and intimate way.

So in the afterlife we can anticipate that God will be there. And we will be there. You will be Todd, an individual, loved by God throughout every stage of your life, and then in that part of life that is called death. So the Apostle Paul insists that each of us will be given a kind of body after we die, much as Jesus appeared to his followers on Easter in such a sure and unmistakable way that they could only say that he came to them in bodily form. This is an important affirmation. After all, having a body is part of what makes us distinct individuals. It's the way we experience life and are known by others. When we die we don't join some "universal life force" or anything so impersonal as that. We are distinct individuals in the next life, much as we are in this life. Paul calls our afterlife body a "spiritual body," a description that still leaves a lot of questions unanswered, but a description that makes clear that we will remain distinct individuals, with individual histories and personalities.

And if God preserves the individual after death, we can expect to encounter others after we die. Jesus said to the thief who was crucified with him, "This day you will be with me in paradise." I will admit that this is hard to picture. For instance, how can the woman with seven husbands possibly sort out all the interweaving relationships?

I have come to some partial understanding of this by comparing it to my memories of Christmas celebrations. When I try to recall any particular Christmas celebration a large assortment of people show up and the tenses get all confused. My father and mother are there. My Aunt Tudy is there, as she was every year after Uncle Edgar died. My grandmother is there, sitting quietly in the corner. In addition to these four, who have all died, you and Alanna, your mother and I, are there as well. Aunt Tudy takes Alanna in her lap to tell her a story, even though she died before Alanna was born. My father delights in your jokes, as surely as he would have if he had lived to meet you.

That is, in this Christmas of my memory all the scattered pieces of life are put together in ways that were never possible in any "real" Christmas. I believe that when I assemble a memory of some Christmas past I catch a fragmentary glimpse of the afterlife. In the afterlife, as in these jumbled Christmas memories, people are united with God and reunited with one another. The tenses get all confused, which is another way of saying that we will be freed from the limits of time. Death no longer will have the power to separate the generations. We will be together in ways that are impossible in this life, and that we can only barely approach in our dreams.

Some people try to dismiss such affirmations by saying that they are just wishful thinking. But they are deeply rooted in what we believe about God. If God cares for each unique individual in a uniquely individual way, then God will not carelessly throw a treasured individual into oblivion. One might imagine a child tossing out a toy in which he has lost interest. But we are not God's toys. We are God's beloved children. You've heard the expression "It's just too good to be true." Well, when we believe in a God who has the power to raise Jesus from the dead and when we believe in a God who values each one as if there were only one, then eternal life is simply too good *not* to be true.

I wish I had more details. I wish, for instance, that I could tell you in what way you will still "get to do stuff" after you die. But I don't know that. Instead, our faith teaches us that God will be there and we will be there as individual personalities. And, most of the time at least, that is enough for me to know, enough for me to leave the details to God, enough for me to respond in wonder and trust.

LOVE, D.

37 · Other Religions

Dear Laura,

One of the stories you can read in the Gospels of Matthew, Mark, or Luke is called "the Transfiguration" (Matt. 17:1–8). In that story Jesus takes three of his disciples, Peter, James, and John, and together they climb to the top of a mountain. At the top something happens. Jesus is "transfigured," filled with dazzling light. He shines so brightly that he hurts the disciples' eyes. It's like looking into the sun.

When they take a peek they see that Jesus has company. He has been joined by two other blazing figures—Moses, the lawgiver, and Elijah, the prophet. There's something wild and fearsome about the whole experience. Maybe because of that, Peter, the chief disciple, calls out to Jesus, saying, "Master, good thing we are here. We can build three little temples, one for you, and two more, one each for Moses and Elijah!" Jesus doesn't say a word in response, but suddenly a voice cracks like thunder from the clouds that swirl about the mountain peak. That voice says, "This is my Son, listen to him." Roughly translated that means, "Silence, you mere mortal man! This is God's doing!"

Peter's idea of building three little temples ("booths" is what it actually says) is an interesting one. Partly, I suspect, the whole experience was scary, and Peter was trying to get a handle on it and on his fright. Besides, building three little shrines would have been a way to mark and remember this amazing encounter with the holy, with God.

Religion is just that—our human response to holiness, to God's revealings. It is what we humans do to mark, to remember, and to get a handle on such experiences. That is why there are so many different religions. Human begins are forever building shrines, temples, systems to mark or capture something that feels powerful, ultimate, holy, or divine. Humanity has more ways to make religion than Burger King ("We let you have it your way!") has of making hamburgers.

Among all the different religions, some have proven constructive, others destructive, and most some of both, depending on the times and who's in charge. Some religions have stood the test of time and have shown themselves able to adapt to changing conditions and needs. These religions that have stood the test of time are sometimes referred to as "the world's great religions." That category usually includes Buddhism, Hinduism, Judaism, Christianity, and Islam, and maybe one or two others, depending on who is making up the list.

My general view is that all of the "great religions" have something to offer and they, along with those who practice them, deserve respect. Our Jewish, Islamic, Hindu, and Buddhist friends and neighbors are part of an important tradition and have things to teach and share with us, just as we, as Christians, have things to teach and share with them.

In one sense, Christianity is but another of the world's great religions. We, too, have our shrines, temples, leaders, systems, and practices. Christianity has spawned its own elaborate networks of institutions, hierarchies, rituals, and practices.

In another sense, Christianity, or the gospel (the Christian message), is a death knell for all religions, our own included. I know that sounds weird, but bear with me for a moment. In a way all the different religions, great and not-so-great, are human systems for getting to God, getting on God's good side, or getting God on our side. Pray this way! Believe this, not that! Behave this way, and not another way! What the Christian gospel, the story of Jesus, says to all our human attempts to get on God's good side, or to get God on our side, is STOP IT! Stop doing all those things to get to God because God has come to you.

Christianity is a religion of grace (see my letter "Grace"), which means, among other things, we do not have to do anything to get to God or to get on God's good side. God comes to our side. It is all about what God has done, and what God has done is a free gift, or grace. A famous South African Christian, Desmond Tutu, puts it this way, "Christianity is not a religion of virtue. It is a religion of grace. Christianity does not say, 'If you are good, then God will love you.' Christianity says, 'We are good because God loves us.'"

Some great theologians have said that Christianity is, in this sense, against religion, if by religion we mean human systems for getting to God, getting on God's good side, or getting a handle on the holy. Those who make this point say that Christianity has overturned religion altogether by saying, "You don't have to do anything to get God to love you. God just does. God has come to us and loves us as a gift of free grace. You can't earn what is a gift. You can only say, 'Thanks!'" They go on to say that basically this is what living as a Christian boils down to, saying thank you.

It doesn't matter, ultimately, whether you worship God on Sunday, as most Christians do, on Saturday as Jews do, Friday with the Muslims, or at the new moon with Buddhists. It doesn't change God's mind one way or the other if you pray, as Catholics do, with a beaded rosary, or like Episcopalians with a prayer book, or like Pentecostals when the spirit strikes you. Any of these or all of these practices may be just fine. But none of them matters ultimately. They are different human responses to God. No more and no less.

In the world we live in today, where there are many different religions, it is terribly important that we study and learn about the main or most influential ones. We need to know how they work, the role they play in different nations and societies, and what they have to contribute. Moreover, as a Christian I believe it is important to respect other faiths and those who practice them. Jesus taught us, "Welcome the stranger."

That said, to be a Christian is to believe that what God has done in Jesus Christ is true, is the truth. God has come to us, embracing human life and experience as God's own. As I've said, this is a free gift—it's grace. To all our systems, religious and otherwise, for getting to God, getting on God's good side, or getting God on our side, God has said, STOP IT! You don't have to do that. I have come to you. I love you. I will never leave you or desert you. Trust this and live. And remember to say thanks.

Love, Dad

Letters about Christianity

38 · Why I Am a Christian

Dear Todd,

Having written letters to you about various aspects of the Christian faith, I want now to write to you about why I am a Christian. I can't answer that question in the same way that I could tell you why I went to the college I did, or why I married your mother. My parents didn't raise me with an expectation and hope that I would go to a particular college and they left the decision of who I would marry entirely up to me. Unlike those decisions, any account of why I am a Christian has to begin with the fact that I was raised in the Christian faith. My parents brought me to the church at a very early age so that I might be baptized. My father is the one who baptized me and, among the things he said as he traced the shape of the cross on my forehead, is "You are marked with the sign of the cross forever." I believe that, in some way, Jesus Christ laid a claim on my life in that moment, as if I were no longer entirely my own person because my life was now bound to his.

Of course, eventually I did have a choice in the matter. I decided to follow Jesus. I also would have been free to choose a different faith or no faith at all. But to begin with my choice would be misleading. Rather, in some real way, I am a Christian because God first chose to claim me in baptism and my parents chose to offer me up to God in this way.

One of the promises my parents made when I was baptized was to raise me in the church. My parents couldn't have compelled me to be a Christian, even if they had wanted to, but one of the things that Christians have learned over the centuries is that a child who is nurtured by a church is better prepared to commit his/her life to Christ. And, as you know, I have spent a great deal of my life in the church, and from a very early age. I suppose God knew that I needed all the help I could get.

Much of my growing up years was spent in the church. I didn't experience many of the difficulties often associated with growing up as a pastor's son. My father didn't burden me with special expectations simply because I was the son of a pastor. Not that I didn't have moments of rebellion. I remember that when I was twelve or so the director of Christian Education of our church came huffing and puffing into our third floor classroom and demanded to know who had thrown a folding chair out the window. Unfortunately, at that point my brother had not yet become a lawyer. I could have used him.

Even as a teenager I liked going to church. Perhaps it had something to do with the fact that our church always had the best dances. The youth group was a major center of social activity. But there were other things, too. I used to love to sit with my mother in worship. I remember that I was usually sleepy on Sunday morning, having stayed up too late the night before. There was something about singing the "Amen" at the end of the hymns that always made me yawn. My mother would look at me and smile, and then we would giggle together, our own little inside joke. I remember those moments perhaps more than anything my father said in a sermon. It made an impression.

I have to be careful in how I express what I want to say next, because it could be easily misunderstood. As much as I enjoyed being in the church, it didn't seem to have all that much to do with God. Remember, this was the fifties and early sixties. In those days every good American citizen was expected to be involved in a church. It was part of the culture. That is, in those days a lot more was assumed—including a basic belief in God. I don't question the faith of my father or anyone else who was a part of the church at that time, but the faith dimension of church life in those days was largely implicit. Faith in God wasn't front and center, but more like an assumed foundation. For instance, there was not a notable reliance on prayer. There wasn't any particular attentiveness to Scripture. The name of Jesus wasn't invoked often, except when he was cited as a peerless teacher of life's lessons.

So the church I grew up in seemed like a gathering of good folks trying to do the right thing. And there is a lot to be said for that. There is always a need for good people who are trying to do the right thing—to raise responsible children, to support one another in times of need, to strengthen the moral fabric of the culture, to address the needs of those less fortunate. Those are all praiseworthy endeavors. But much of the time while growing up I got the impression—perhaps unfairly—that it didn't have all that much to do with God. That is, if there were no God we might have found ourselves doing many of the same things anyway.

On my college applications I said that I intended to be a lawyer. I immersed myself in college life. I didn't go to church. It was probably the furthest thing from my mind. But I have learned that God can be sneaky and resourceful. Looking back, God was chasing me down, even in college, of all places. I took a religion course to fulfill a requirement and I was surprised by how much it engaged me. Then I took another and another.

Then a surprising thing happened. The chaplain of the college—who didn't know me—asked me if I would be interested in working Sundays with the youth program of a church in a nearby city. One of the religion professors had suggested I might be interested. At the time I did not see this as I do now, as an example of our sneaky and resourceful God yanking me back into the church. No, God is too sneaky to be that obvious. At the time I remember thinking that the fifty dollars a week they were offering in salary would sure help and it did occur to me, even then, that it would be nice to be back in a church again.

I had a good experience there, enough to embolden me to apply to seminary. That was not an easy decision to make. I didn't know much about what a call to ministry is, but I was quite sure that it wasn't like going into the family business. Even as I was packing my bags to go to seminary, I still didn't know how to explain to myself or others why I would do such a thing.

I remember being anxious that the only people I would meet in seminary would be religious nerds. So I was particularly wary when, my first week there, another first-year student who lived down the hall asked me if I wanted to join in a small prayer group. I was a minister's son, a religion major in college who for two years was on the staff of a church, and I still didn't have any real experience in prayer. Up to that point, I hadn't known anyone who was part of a prayer group, except a few folks in college who gathered, I suspected at the time, in a prayer group because they couldn't get a date. I expressed some of my skepticism to this fellow student and then I agreed to give it a try.

This little handful of people ended up meeting every week for four years. They were not religious nerds, I was relieved to find, but some of the most engaging, interesting, fun people I have ever known. They are some of the best friends I have ever had. We shared joys and concerns, prayed together about them, and promised to remember them daily in our individual prayers throughout the week. This kind of prayer is not something I ever learned in my home church or even in my family. As strange as this seemed to me at first, every time we gathered we would go over the list we compiled the previous week and ask, "What does God seem to be doing here since we last met?" It was amazing to me how often even I was able to see God at work and, of course, often in surprising ways. In those years this little group shared much laughter and many tears. During our years together, three of us became engaged and married, another was divorced, another came to the understanding that he is gay, and the father of another was imprisoned for embezzling money. And God was powerfully at work. Rather than growing in my skepticism about prayer, I became awestruck at its power.

At the same time, while I was in seminary, I was working in another church, largely with the youth. In addition to the usual youth group activities, I tried offering a Bible study. Somewhat to my surprise, the youth dove in with an enthusiasm that is usually reserved for the latest trend. In fact, this was something new for them. They were stunningly ignorant of the Bible (one evening I discovered that fully half of them had never heard the story about Moses and the burning bush), but in some ways that was a distinct advantage. Reading the Bible with fresh eyes, they responded to it as if it were both very odd and surprisingly interesting. This was strange, exotic stuff, and gathering to read it each week seemed off-center enough to appeal to the counter-cultural impulses of these teenagers. Reading the Bible with them I saw, as if for the first time, the power in this story, so much more heady, radical, and mysterious than my experience in either the church or school had led me to believe.

And somewhere along the line, in ways I cannot trace fully, Jesus became very real to me. Jesus became a living presence to me, rather than just a figure in history. Jesus became someone to know, rather than merely learn about. I began to speak of him in the present tense and the future tense, as well as the past tense, because I experienced him as alive and at work in the world. Somehow it became clear to me that everything depends on him. Jesus is the one who makes God real to me.

As I say, I don't know how that happened exactly, or even much about when it happened. But it has something to do with hanging around in the church for as long as I have. That is not to be assumed, of course. Many people find that the church's flaws and failings hide Jesus more than reveal Jesus; for them, the church is the last place they might expect to encounter God. And there are ways in which being a pastor can be ruinous to your spiritual life because we are often the ones who see the flaws and failings most clearly. But I was found by God in the church, of all places.

I think I may have been called into parish ministry in part because I needed more time than some to see God and hear God. I've spent a long time in the church. It has taken a long time. But now I see the Spirit of Christ at work every day, and in the church, of all places. And sometimes it's almost overwhelming, like being able to hear the grass grow would be overwhelming at times.

Of course God is at work outside the church. But that never struck me as surprising. The astonishing discovery of my life is that God can be at work abundantly and tangibly in the church. And somehow God has been sneaky enough and resourceful enough to keep me hanging around the church long enough to see it—that is, long enough to see God and to be blessed by the sight.

I suppose there are people who can be content with less. For them, life is about having a good job and a nice home, doing some good deeds, making some friends, going on a few trips, perhaps having a couple of children, avoiding pain whenever possible, and seeking pleasure wherever they can find it. And I want many of those things for my life as well. But add all of that together and it still seems rather meager to me. Such a purpose is not large enough, strong enough, or enduring enough to bear the weight of a human life. As a Christian, however, I find my life caught up in a larger story about God's enduring love affair with the world. To take even a small part in that drama gives my life meaning.

And I have found the Christian story to be true—true in the fullest sense of being trustworthy. I have tested it not only with my mind but, more importantly, with my whole life. It is a story that keeps making sense out of my life. My own faith may be fickle, but God's faithfulness endures. So even when I stumble or fall, I experience the truth that underneath it all are the everlasting arms of God.

When you love someone as much as I love you, it means a great deal to be able to entrust you to the care of the God I have found to be so trustworthy. When you were little you would sometimes call out to us in the middle of the night because you had a nightmare, and sometimes I was the one who came to your room to comfort you. Sometimes your fears were easily handled. You would say, "Daddy, I think there are bears in my closet." And I would say, "No, there are no bears." "How do you know?" "I'll turn on the light and you'll see." But there were other times when you didn't want any words of reassurance. You would ask, "Just stay with me." And I would stay with you. I might be a bit sleepy, but I loved being able to sit with you. It felt wonderful to be able to protect you from whatever was frightening you just by holding vigil like that.

Then one night you asked another question: "Will you stay with me no matter what?" I don't remember what I said in response, but I probably assured you that I would not leave. What I do remember very clearly, however, is how unsettling your question was. I knew that I would stay with you that night and, if need be, many other nights in the future. But I also knew that there would come a time—perhaps a night many years later, a night much darker than any you had yet experienced, a night when you would face dangers more real and more frightening than bears in your closet—when you would need me and I would not be there or I would not be able to help. That night, as you finally drifted back to sleep, I became aware, as I have many times since, of how grateful I am that I can entrust your life to the God I have found to be trustworthy, the One who I know will stand by you, uphold you, strengthen you, and comfort you, no matter what, in times and in ways I cannot. And because I love you so much, that realization makes me love God all the more.

Love, D.

(Martin)

39 · Why I Am a Christian

Dear Laura,

A writer whose books I like answered a question similar to this one by making a distinction between two different kinds of things. The first he called "causes," and the second "reasons." By "causes" he meant factors in his background and the society in which he grew up that had *caused* or influenced him to be a Christian. But at some point these background factors and influences were not enough. They were not the whole answer. He had to have *reasons*, his own reasons for being a Christian.

Although that writer is a generation older than I am and grew up in Canada rather than the United States, his two parts seem a good way to approach this question for me as well. Like him I was born into a family and a society that were "Christian" in much the same way that we were "American." That is, these things were a given, not exactly like having blue or brown eyes, but close.

When I was growing up there was very little of the diversity of religions and faiths that is common today. Today, the question someone might ask is, "If you are a religious person, what is your faith?" Forty years ago, the question was different. Then the question was, "Are you a Protestant or a Catholic?" Those were the two major types of Christians. If you answered "Protestant," then there might be a follow-up question, "What type?" meaning, which denomination? Presbyterian, Methodist, Baptist, Lutheran, Episcopalian, and Congregational were the most common.

Most families went to one Christian church or another, and our family was no exception. Not only did most people think of themselves (perhaps without thinking about it much) as "Christian," but also Christian language and symbols permeated the world in which I grew up. Stores were closed on Sundays, and there were no kid's soccer games on Sundays either. It was the Christian Sabbath. Teachers often began the school day with a prayer and sometimes a reading from the Bible. School and community Christmas pageants and programs included the singing of Christian songs and carols. Church services and programs were regularly on television and radio.

I am sure that this all sounds pretty strange, certainly different, to you. And yet it was this way in most parts of the United States less than fifty years ago. This taken-for-granted Christianity was, I've come to believe, a mixed blessing at best. Anytime that something (in this case Christianity) is everywhere, it is also in an odd way, nowhere. Or to put it another way, when something is taken for granted it may not be very deeply or carefully considered.

Still, a form of Christianity was in the air I breathed and the water I drank, so to speak, as I grew up. This changed, quite rapidly, in my own teenage and young adult years. It was the sixties (you'll read about this someday in a history book, if you haven't already), and everything that had once been taken for granted was now questioned. And I mean everything. Government and presidents, citizenship and patriotism, sex and marriage, religion and parents.

Our society went from taking everything for granted to taking nothing for granted. How that happened is a complicated matter that I am not sure anyone fully understands even yet. It had a lot to do with the Vietnam War, but many other things too. Looking back, both extremes—accepting everything you've been given and rejecting everything you've been given—both seem equally unwise.

But the questioning of the sixties and seventies meant that the Christianity that most people had taken for granted as they grew up, and which I had taken for granted, was now questioned, challenged, and often rejected. Such questioning was (and is) not a bad thing. In fact, it is a good thing. Any faith that is going to count for much, or see you through hard times, has to be able to stand up to questions.

I, too, went through a time of questioning and a phase of rejecting the faith in which I had grown up. What brought me back to the church and the Christian faith, or in a real way, led me to find out what it was all about for the first time for myself? What, in other words, and to return to the framework I mentioned at the beginning, were the *reasons* I found to be a Christian when the *causes* wore thin and were no longer convincing?

In another of my letters to you, you will learn that I had a strong sense of something beyond myself and of some larger purpose and meaning at work in the world. In the 1970s, as the energy and excitement of the sixties began to wane, many people seemed to have lost this sense of a larger purpose or meaning to life—of being a part of something greater than only themselves. Maybe I had lost some of that myself. Maybe that sense of loss, or hunger, led me to reconsider religion, and specifically the Christian faith.

As I did reconsider it and came to the Christian faith as a young adult, there were two crucial entry points for me. One was a small, racially mixed (white and African American) congregation where I was drawn to people whose faith was real and honest. Their faith gave joy to their lives, which they lived out on a day-to-day basis. The other point of entry for me was the Bible. For the first time, I found myself really reading and studying the Bible. I found that it was not just a book of rules or advice about how to be a good person. I wasn't much interested in that anyhow. What I found instead was a book full of strange and wonderful stories—stories about men and women and their encounters with "something greater" than themselves—with the one the Bible called, "God" and "Spirit."

Through both of these—a particular community and the Bible—I experienced that larger power and purpose that I had long sensed and sought. It was as if I was meeting, or being met by, that something or someone through the life of that congregation and its people, and through the Bible. These two experiences helped me see other ways in which God was at work in my life and in the world.

In time, I began to see that the Bible is not just a batch of different stories, but that it is also one big story, with many, many parts. It is the story of God, of a God who surprises people, who creates new beginnings, and who breaks in when the world (or a part of it) is too stuck or settled or closed or hopeless.

These ways of God I came to understand and name. "Grace" was the word for it. It is a word that means gift. It was grace when God led the Hebrew slaves through the Red Sea to freedom. It was grace when manna rained down in the wilderness so that they had something to eat. It was grace when Jesus was born in a manger in the midst of a dark and scary world. It was grace when the stone was rolled away from the tomb. It is grace when it snows. It is grace when someone loves you, and when you love someone. It is usually grace when opportunity knocks, and grace when you have the courage to answer.

I was, and am, someone who expects a lot of himself and of others. That's a good thing, but most good things can become bad things if they are taken too far or pushed too hard. When you expect a lot of yourself you can become almost driven and you can become quite demanding. I needed a way to balance this part of my life and personality. I found it in this story about God. I found it in grace. Grace and the faith enabled me to see that God was real and trustworthy and it showed me that it wasn't all on my shoulders or up to me. I had a part in the play, but I wasn't the playwright or even the director.

It took longer for me to come to know Jesus, partly because I was put off and made uncomfortable by at least some of those who claimed to know him best. They were altogether too sure, too certain, and sometimes seemed a little phony.

For me, getting to know Jesus started with the cross. Like everyone, I had known some difficulties and had, by then, seen some suffering and death. In the cross I saw that Jesus (and the Christian faith) did not try to run away from suffering or pretend it didn't exist. To me, the cross said that God, in Jesus, accepted suffering as part of life, embraced it in a way, and so embraced everyone who suffered. This was different than what I often saw. Often it seemed that people turned away from suffering and from those who suffered. In embracing suffering in this way, Jesus also changed it. The cross showed that suffering, pain, and evil were real, but they did not have the last word. The last word, which in a way is also the first word, is God and grace and new life.

Then I began to notice more. I noticed how strange, really, and how challenging were the stories about Jesus and also how wonderfully odd his own stories and teachings are. He was not just a really nice or even just a really loving guy. He was more than that, for his love and his way were incredibly challenging to me, challenging in a good way. When you pay attention to him, as he comes to us in the Gospels, he almost always sees life and people in a different light and way. To me his way of seeing has the ring of truth. More and more I found myself challenged and disturbed, again in a good way, by who he was and is. He went beyond, and took me beyond, just trying to be a good person to something more, to living with a surprising and grace-full God.

In time I came to see that Jesus was the real basis for questioning the taken-for-granted world of my childhood and youth, but not only that. Jesus is the basis for questioning all of taken-for-granted stuff. He is the basis for questioning and challenging every human order that diminishes or distorts life, that makes it less than what God meant it to be. He has taken me on a lifelong journey of faith, hope, and love. But it is a journey that is different in one crucial respect from any other journey. That one difference is this: he goes with me on this journey. In Jesus I find a sure companion from whom nothing can separate me (not the world's best or worst nor my own best or worst). I find in him a continuing challenge and a constant grace. That is why I am a Christian.

LOVE, DAD

(Tony)

Afterword

DEAR TODD,

In the summer of 2004, a year after the original edition of this book was published, you and I traveled to the Pacific Northwest. While we were there, we went on an overnight backpacking trip with Tony and Laura. Tony was eager to share with us some of the beauty of that part of the country and we all thought it would be fun for the four of us—the principle characters in this book—to spend some time together. Up until then, Tony and I had spent a good deal of time together over the years, but you and Laura had only met once.

As we prepared for the backpacking trip, I knew we were in good hands. You and I have had only a bit of experience with backpacking, but Tony and Laura clearly were pros. They had all the right equipment for themselves and enough on hand to outfit us, as well. We headed out to Goats Rocks Wilderness Area in the Cascade Mountain Range under clear blue skies. Tony assured us that he had picked out a trail with some spectacular scenery. He particularly thought that we would love the dramatic views of Mount Adams from that trail.

By the time we left the car at the head of the trail and started walking, the skies had turned overcast. A rather thick fog had crept in, as well. We could not see much beyond the line of trees or the open fields that were nearest to the trail. Every so often, Tony would say, "This is a spectacular view right here. I wish you could see it." Or, "This is perhaps my favorite vista. Too bad there is so much fog." He expressed awe at the sights we could not see: "Mount Adams, if you could see it, has this gorgeous peak that juts up into the sky right here," and he attempted to trace the outline of the peak with his finger to help us visualize it. I trust Tony's judgment enough to be sure that we missed some of the most beautiful scenery we have never seen.

When we got to the place where we were to spend the night, we set up our tents and cooked dinner together. By the time dinner was ready a light rain began to fall. The four of us stood under the only shelter big enough for the four of us—the outstretched branches of a large tree. Before we finished our dinner, the rain became quite steady. It was still early, but the only sensible option was for us to repair to our tents.

Tony and Laura, both avid readers, had brought paperbacks to read. They even had special flashlights that strapped to their heads so they could read into the night. So they were quite content to crawl into their tent and enjoy their books. You and I, of course, had no books and only a single hand-held flashlight. You turned to me and said, "So what are we going to do now, Dad? Tell manly stories?" I don't remember if that is what we did (I'm not even sure I know any "manly stories"), but I do remember listening to the rain and laughing at our predicament.

The next morning we headed back on the same trail we had come in on. For the hike out there was a bit less fog and a whole lot more rain. Once again Tony pointed out the sights we were mostly unable to see. We agreed that we could see at least the outlines of Mount Adams. Or perhaps Tony's descriptions were so vivid that we only thought we could see it.

I have thought back on that time together quite often through the years. I have concluded that it is even something of a metaphor for what we have tried to do with this book. We have tried to point out some things along the way: things that are important to us, that we think are impressive or beautiful. I'm not sure you could always see what we were pointing to. Perhaps there were times when you have felt as if you were looking at mere fog. But my hope has been, and continues to be, that as we spend more time on the trail together you might see—or at least imagine—some of the landscape I know so well and love so dearly. After all, you want to share the things you most care about with the people you love.

AND I LOVE YOU VERY MUCH, D.

CPSIA information can be obtained
at www.ICGtesting.com
Printed in the USA
BVHW051831180522
637434BV00016B/138